AUTH

ADVANCED PUBLISHING AND MARKETING STRATEGIES FOR INDIE AUTHORS

SELF-PUBLISHING GUIDE BOOK ONE

Robert J. Ryan

Cover design by 187designz

ISBN: 9781697053975
(print edition)

Trotting Fox Press

Contents

Introduction
Who am I to Give Advice?
1. The Most Important Tool to Sell Books?
2. How Pro Marketers Structure Blurbs
3. Seven Blurb Myths That Kill Sales
4. Covers and Eye-Tracking Technology
5. The Types of Titles that Sell
6. How Continuity Fuels the Sales Engine
7. The Secrets in Plain Sight
8. How the Pros Write to Market
9. Why Great Books Fail
10. Minimum Viable Product Theory Debunked
11. The Science of Purchase Psychology
12. What Amazon Ads do that Other Ads Can't
13. Amazon Ads: How Real Gurus Make Money
14. Is There a Future for Indie Publishing?
15. A Candid Appraisal of Indie Resources
16. A Facebook Group to Seek out Best Practice

Introduction

This is the truth.

Amazon's Kindle Store is massive. It already contains millions of titles, and thousands of new books are added daily – perhaps hourly. Many of them are good. They all fight for their light under the sun, and competition is brutal. Added to that, Amazon is increasingly a pay-to-play platform.

Fighting for visibility in those conditions is like Bambi shaping up to Godzilla. Godzilla on steroids.

But this is another truth. It's less well known, but grasp it and it'll give you strength.

Despite the difficulties, people succeed. Many of them are veterans of indie publishing. But quite a lot are new.

There are ways to rise from under the shadow of competition, and to feel the sun on your face. There are ways to make a full-time living at this business. Every day, people quit their jobs to do so.

What do they know? What are their skillsets? How is it they do what others can't?

There are answers to those questions. I've learned a few of them. I continue to learn more. At any rate, I had learned enough by March 2, 2018, to quit my job. I've been a full-time author since then, and I wish I'd done it sooner.

I want you to have your own March 2.

And that's what this book is about. I'm passing on, without holding anything back, what I've learned.

This is not a beginner's book. If you're looking for an introduction to indie publishing, I recommend starting with something like David Gaughran's *Let's Get Digital*.

This is a book of advanced strategies and tactics. Even veterans with a large backlist will learn quite a few things that they wouldn't expect. But it's also for those who've published several times without the success they want. Or, perhaps, that highly select group who haven't published yet, but who take this business seriously and are tirelessly preparing to make the best start possible.

For them, I offer this advice. All the hard work in the world isn't enough. That labor must be guided by correct knowledge, or the effort is lost.

When you finish this book, please tell me if you think I've given you that knowledge.

Who am I to Give Advice?

It's a good question. It's *the* question. Here's my answer.

Before I quit my job, I worked for the government. Try not to hold a grudge against me. What I did there revolved around ensuring people complied with legislative requirements.

Worse, they were *tax* requirements.

Still holding that grudge at bay? But perhaps you begin to see why March 2 was a special day. Raising revenue for the government is a soul-crushing job.

Enough of that. My core task back then was ensuring people complied with legislation ... and often people would rather *not*. This is a problem all governments face, and not just for tax. As a result, they employ teams of people with copywriting, behavioral economics, behavioral insight and marketing skillsets. Their brief? Persuade people to do the right thing. Or at least what the legislation says is the right thing...

I was one of them. I was a persuader.

You might be surprised how seriously some government departments take this. They do so because in their world things are done on scale. Sending out a letter? That's not a walk down to the local post office. A single mail out might be fifty thousand at a time. All of a sudden, a letter that gets a 1% improvement in response rate saves the government a fortune in administrative expenses. It means fewer follow-up letters. It means fewer phone calls. And more people understanding and meeting their obligations. Governments just love that.

My department took it so seriously that we had access to regular focus groups, a support network across interstate and multijurisdictional lines and novelties like infrared eye-tracking technology. This technology allows research into how people read a web page, how they read a letter and what they look at and don't look at. We used every tool at our disposal to monitor what worked, and what didn't.

That's what I did. And I specialized in copywriting techniques. Others I worked with included behavioral psychologists, qualitative market research scientists and behavioral economists. We learned off each other and pooled our skills together to get the job done.

My work covered a wide field. Letters. Websites. Strategic advice on communication methods. Drafting ads for industry journals. Advising on training methods. Providing lectures to staff on the basic principles of copywriting. Heading a video project and drafting the script for it. Interesting stuff (but not as much fun as writing fiction).

Not long before I left, I won the department's inaugural innovation challenge. And (you guessed it) that was off the back of a copywriting concept.

Okay. I've risked boring your socks off with this government stuff for a reason. Everything I was doing for my day job was fertile training for my next job – transforming myself from a part-time to a full-time indie publisher.

Now that's a job I don't have to apologize for.

My fiction is published under a pen name as well as my real name – Robert Ryan. For nonfiction, I insert a J.

And what have I achieved as an indie author? Long story short: freedom. I work for myself. I'm my own boss, and I earn a comfortable living. Comfortable enough that part of my writing schedule involves a post-lunch nana nap. Something that none of my copywriting skills ever convinced a government boss to approve. Go figure.

Now, your goals may not be the same as mine. If not, I urge you to at least consider the nana nap. But whatever they are, I'm pretty sure they involve finding ways to take your fiction-writing craft and infuse it with publishing expertise and marketing savvy so you can break out and reach the next level.

It can be done. I've done it. I know what you want to know, and the rest of this book provides that knowledge.

1. The Most Important Tool to Sell Books?

It's the blurb.

I'll explain why I say that in a moment, but first I'll bust one of the biggest myths out there. It's a myth people believe because it sounds right. But it isn't, no matter that it's promoted by a tiny group of "gurus" following outdated tactics never even intended for book buyers.

And if you're following this advice, it's costing you sales and annoying readers.

We're often told that a blurb is sales copy, and that its purpose is to sell the book. Because it's sales copy, it should have a buy call to action (CTA) like some other ads. Probably these ads are in the minority these days anyway because modern copywriters use more sophisticated tactics than the stale and annoying "buy now" command. Time was when the passive-aggressive "buy now" order actually worked on a percentage of the public. It still does now, but only in limited situations and it has to be deployed correctly.

This buy CTA business is close to the mark. Dangerously close. But *close* to the mark isn't professional. It's not good enough. Marketing is a tough business. Close enough is often the difference between success and failure. A brain surgeon doesn't get close enough when they operate. They get it right, or the results are catastrophic. It's not as bad in marketing, but getting it wrong loses you money and steals away your dreams.

So, to explain further, a blurb is sales copy. It's not fiction. It's not a story synopsis. It's an integral part of the sales funnel. Now, there are various descriptions for how the sales funnel works, but they all go something like this:

Awareness of the product
Evaluation of the product
Interest is stimulated
Interest transforms into desire
Action occurs (buy or don't buy)

It's that last part that concerns us here. In marketing, the person moving through the sales funnel is termed the "prospect" which is short for "prospective buyer". And the end point of a sales funnel is when the prospect makes the decision of whether or not to buy.

Enter the CTA. It's used at just this point. Like a finely tuned machine, it goes to work at the precise moment the prospect is on the cusp of making the buy/don't buy decision. Its purpose? Firstly, to offer a final nudge to help the prospect over the line. Secondly, it makes it easy for the prospect to know exactly what to *do* in order to buy.

This is why "buy now" is such a frequently seen link at the end of a digital ad. It's never "If you've decided you may like this product, please keep reading and we'll explain how to go about buying it."

Not a bit of that. Too long winded. Too wishy washy.

"Buy now" does work. So does "Subscribe now" or "Donate now." It depends on the ad because not everything is a sale. But whatever it is, the language usually includes an imperative verb, and at least in digital advertising, it's a clickable link. So, "Buy now with 1 click" is both the CTA and the means to buy the product.

Neat, huh?

So, why is this blurb advice to put a buy CTA at the end wrong? Well, put yourself in the shoes of the prospect. In this case, when they're reading the blurb, you have to consider where they're mentally positioned in the sales funnel.

This is critical. If you deploy the CTA too early, it's wasted. People don't buy when they're in the evaluation stage. They're still evaluating. It's like a waiter asking diners what they're ordering to eat – before they've seen the menu. That's ineffective timing. Not to mention annoying. And that's the very last thing you want.

Back to the prospect. Where are they in the sales funnel when they reach the end of the blurb? Just like the diners, they're in the restaurant. They may even be seated. But they *haven't* read the menu yet. They're still in the evaluation phase, not the action phase.

For prospective book buyers, the menu could be the reviews. Or it could be the preview feature. It's probably both. Deploying a buy CTA before they've finished evaluating … is ineffective and annoying. Worse, it steals power from the end of a blurb like kryptonite makes Superman's knees weak.

Amazon doesn't give us data about what percentage of people look at reviews and what percentage read the preview. But we know massive number of people do both.

The end of the blurb is therefore a crossroads. Five main things remain possible. The reader could click away, uninterested. They could buy. They could click on an also-bought or an ad. They could check out reviews. Or they could decide to read the preview.

We don't know what percentage of people do each of these things. But Amazon does. They have hundreds of millions of statistical datapoints of what people do at that juncture. If they wanted, they could put a buy CTA right at the end of the blurb. If their statistics showed that was where the evaluation stage shifted into the action stage, they *would*.

But they don't. Interesting, don't you think?

The buy button is instead at the top of the page. But there has to be one there. People might buy off a cover click (rarely). Much more likely, they're following a link from someplace like BookBub or Goodreads (where they've already read a blurb and looked at review stats). They're either going to buy straight up (because they've shifted through the evaluation stage on the other site), or click the cover to look inside. Both options are handily placed together at the top of the page.

Where then is the other main buy CTA positioned? At the very end of the preview. And what they have there is a pretty blue link that says, imperative verb and all, "Buy now with 1-Click."

Amazon, probably the best marketers in the world, know where to place and word a buy CTA. And they don't put it at the end of the blurb, but at the end of the preview.

All this begs a question. If we shouldn't place a buy CTA at the end of a blurb, what *should* we put there?

What traditional publishers put there. Like Amazon, they know a thing or two about marketing. They finish the blurb with a nice, juicy cliffhanger style story hook.

If you want, you can call this a passive CTA. It stimulates the reader's desire to keep going down the sales funnel. It impels them along their own personal buying path, and it doesn't matter in the least if that's reviews or the preview. It does the job the same, either way.

I've gone into this in detail. It's a fairly small thing really, but it pinpoints how deeply you need to think about these things.

The difference between selling well and not selling well is a bunch of smaller choices like this all coming together. This is the professional mindset required to succeed. It's how you take the next step. It's how you move beyond the standard advice. Because the standard advice is what everyone's doing.

Dig deeper. Find the truth. Standard practice is not enough. You want *best* practice. In everything. Get *all* your ducks in a row, and things start to look after themselves – allowing you time for those nana naps.

Right. I promised earlier to explain why the blurb is your most important tool to sell books. So, let's look into that. Carefully. Digging deep for the truth.

I'm not for a moment forgetting the value of covers. Or marketing such as newsletter promotions or Amazon, Facebook or BookBub ads. But the blurb is the most important factor. And this is why.

The blurb is like the hub at the center of a wagon wheel. All the spokes lead to it, or from it. It's where everybody comes to start exploring the book. It's the point where true evaluation begins.

Remember the sales funnel? Covers and advertising bring people to a book's product page. They're the product awareness part, and critical in their way. But anyone can pay for advertising to raise awareness. It's what happens in the evaluation stage that takes true skill. This is where interest is nurtured and turned into desire.

Think about those words. Awareness. Interest. Desire. Which is the more powerful? If your blurb doesn't invoke desire, all that has gone before is in vain.

And while it's true that the blurb isn't the end of the sales funnel, and it's not the action part, it's the hardest mountain of all to climb. The awareness phase is (relatively) easy. The conversion phase where the reader clicks "buy" is (relatively) easy. At least, if you've created desire beforehand. Once you've invoked desire, the reader is most of the way there. They're using reviews and reading the preview for *confirmation* that this is the book for them.

So, how do you turn interest into desire? The next chapter discusses exactly that.

2. How Pro Marketers Structure Blurbs

What creates desire?

This is the holy grail of the advertising world. Some of the smartest marketers on the planet have put their mind to the question. And guess what? They know the answer.

Emotion.

Emotion in advertising is key. Ever wonder why so many ads have cute animals? Because we respond to cuteness on an emotional level. Wonder why Coca-Cola runs slogans like "Taste the Feeling"? Or why the McDonald's slogan is "I'm Lovin' it"?

Emotion isn't always in a slogan, but it often is. And if it's not in the slogan, you can bet it's somewhere else in the ad.

Emotion is the alchemist's elixir that takes interest and transmutes it into desire.

Please don't take my word on this stuff. Take nobody's word on this stuff. Verify it yourself. A Google search along the lines of "importance of emotion in advertising" will do the trick.

So, how can indie authors use this knowledge to create a good blurb?

Pretty simply. There are exceptions to this, but generally no emotion is evoked more quickly than sympathy. Most people are highly empathic. We generally don't fall in love instantly, or hate instantly, but we can feel overwhelming waves of sympathy for a complete stranger in seconds. It's just how humans are wired.

Lots of emotions can work in fiction, but they take *time* to set up and develop. You don't have time in a blurb. You have seconds. Sympathy is a gold-class shortcut.

Bonus points if you make your character likeable at the same time. If you like someone, and you feel sympathy for them ... well, that's rocket fuel for emotion. And blurbs.

But emotion within a blurb doesn't exist in a vacuum. You need a structure to contain it. You need to lead the reader through from the first word of the blurb to the last.

There are popular formulas out there that offer a structure. But they've been handed around among writers. Copywriters wouldn't touch them with a ten-foot pole.

Let's look at the most common variation of the writers' formula, and then what's wrong with it.

Who is the hero?
What does he/she want?
What is the conflict?
What must the hero do?
What is at stake?

There's nothing wrong with this at an informational level. All of these things are good things to have in a blurb. But it's utterly lacking a *marketing* structure, and this will leak sales like a sieve leaks water.

Here, by contrast, is an actual copywriting formula. It's called AIDA, and it's probably the most common and successful sales formula the world has ever seen.

Attention
Interest
Desire
Action

See how it aligns with the marketing sales funnel? That's no accident. It aligns with it because it takes advantage of it every step of the way. Like the sales funnel, it's psychologically in tune with what goes on in a prospect's mind at each stage of the buying process. It's hardwired to sell, which the writers' formula is not.

It's worth noting at this point that there's only one sales funnel. But digital marketing is a little different from old-school marketing. In newspapers and magazines, the whole ad is in one place. The sales funnel is therefore in the same place. Not so with digital advertising.

In digital advertising, the prospect is usually moved from one webpage to another. On Amazon, this might be a bestseller list where a cover seizes their attention. Click. Now they read a blurb and evaluate. Click. Now they're reading the preview and desire turns into an action. Click.

This separation means that each of these pages can be considered their own mini sales funnel. Each starts with an attention phase and ends with an action phase.

Why is all this important?

Back to blurbs. Their mini sales funnel begins with attention because the moment a reader clicks on a cover and gets taken to your book's blurb, the blurb is fighting to keep it. "It" is attention. And attention is fleeting. It's fleeting everywhere, but this fleetingness is magnified to the power of 10 in the digital advertising world.

At this point, the fate of the world (or at least of your book) stands upon the edge of a knife. You have only a matter of *seconds* to reassure the reader they're onto a good thing, and that they should invest further time. Bore them, and they're gone. Confuse them, and they're gone. Send them the wrong signals about genre, and they're gone. They'll click on the shiny new cover of some dolled-up also-bought quicker than a bad boy billionaire sets his sights on the shy college graduate in his office.

This is critical stuff. For verification, Google something like "digital marketing attention span". You have only a matter of seconds to turn attention into interest and keep the prospect in the funnel. This is why internet marketers spend so much time perfecting email subject lines. Fail at this point, and read-through rates of emails (or in our case blurbs) plummet. When read-through rates plummet, sales plunge too.

How, then, do you get attention? Well, this is the main reason blurbs have taglines. And they're usually bolded because that draws the eye. But the content has to draw them in, too. It's often a teaser (an open loop in marketing terms) that poses some sort of question. But it's often not.

Here's an example. It's the opening of the blurb for Robert Ludlum's *The Scarlatti Inheritance.*

The Third Reich is in its death struggle ... A spellbinding story of international terror and intrigue, greed and cunning, suspense and murder from the No. 1 bestselling master storyteller.

Not much in the way of an open loop there. (More on the myth that a hook has to pose a question later). So why is it good? Why can I tell at a glance that a great copywriter drafted it?

If you're an editor, and you're screaming at me right now that this is all telling and not showing, you're right. But keep in mind this is sales copy and not fiction. Sales copy has its own rules, and they're proven to work. Keep the sales copy to a blurb and fiction rules to fiction.

The best way to get someone's attention is to give them something they want. If someone browsing for historical thrillers clicks into this blurb, the tagline lets them know they hit the motherlode. Pretty much everything about it is screaming genre: *The Third Reich. International terror. Intrigue. Suspense. Murder.*

That alone probably seals the deal. Interested in this genre? You'll read on.

But the copywriting works in layers. The next is social proof. *No. 1 bestselling master storyteller.* This lets you know the author is massively popular. And if he's so popular, he's probably good. This is extra impetus to keep reading.

But there's more. Remember we talked about emotion being the key to sales copy? Let's list the words here that invoke emotion. *Death struggle. Spellbinding. Terror. Greed. Murder.*

Wrap all those layers of copywriting up into an opening paragraph, and you have something that will drive a reader of the genre forward.

The next step is interest. This part of the funnel starts to provide specifics. Not a lot, but just enough. This is some element of the plot. It draws the reader deeper into the story. It offers a tiny bit of space to flesh out the hero and help us feel emotion for them. It should continue to reinforce genre, too.

Here's another example. It's the second paragraph of the blurb for Bella Andre's *The Look of Love*.

Chloe Peterson is having a bad night. A really bad night. And when her car skids off the side of a wet country road straight into a ditch, she's convinced even the gorgeous guy who rescues her in the middle of the rain storm must be too good to be true. Or is he?

What's going on here from a copywriting perspective? Again, it's working in layers. Firstly, it's signaling genre quite strongly (romance). It also introduces us to the main character, and straightaway it's giving us a reason to feel sympathy for her. *Chloe Peterson is having a bad night.* Hot on the heels of that ... *her car skids off the side of a wet country road straight into a ditch* ... a bad night indeed.

What else is the blurb writer doing? Well, this is what the blurb writer is doing – dangling a genre-relevant hook at the end of the paragraph to entice us to keep reading. And this time the hook is an open loop (teaser) ... *the gorgeous guy who rescues her in the middle of the rain storm must be too good to be true. Or is he?*

Depending how you look at it, this last bit isn't just a hook. It's also invoking emotion in us again. We feel hope that Chloe might be meeting the man of her dreams, but we also feel worry that she isn't.

Next in the sales funnel is desire. I have to quote in full here because the desire and action elements toward the end of the blurb are built on what precedes them. This is the blurb for Wilbur Smith's *Desert God*.

On the shores of the Nile, the fate of a kingdom rests in one hero's hands...

When the ancient kingdom of Egypt comes under threat, the Pharaoh turns to Taita – freed slave, poet, philosopher and his most trusted advisor – to finally defeat their historic enemy, the Hyksos.

Taita has a cunning plan that will not only deliver a crushing blow to the Hyksos, but will also form a coveted alliance with Crete. In charge of the Pharaoh's sisters Tehuti and Bekatha as well as a mighty army, Taita embarks on a perilous journey up the Nile, through Arabia to the magical city of Babylon, and across the seas.

But beyond battle and betrayal, there is another danger – the spirited young princesses' attraction to two of the warriors leading the fight could not only ruin Taita's plan but threaten the future of Egypt itself.

There's a lot to be learned from that blurb, but I'll stick to commenting about the desire element of the sales funnel.

Desire is grounded in interest. As we learn more of Taita, and of the world in which he lives, that interest increases. At least, if this is your kind of story it does.

Without describing the plot, we learn more of what's happening and what's at stake. Sentence by sentence, we become invested. Desire doesn't operate like attention. Attention is superficial. Desire is deeper, and it goes hand in hand with emotion. And we have emotion at the end, quite strongly. *Betrayal. Danger. Spirited. Attraction. Ruin. Threaten.* All words that invoke emotion. All coming at the end, and all the more powerful now that we know a little of Taita (who comes across as pretty darn likeable). When we reach the end of the blurb, we want Taita to win. To win, and defeat the threat to Egypt itself.

I'll use the same blurb to talk about action.

What do we want the prospect to do at the end of the blurb? Buying would be oh so nice from an author's point of view. But as discussed above, we know most people won't at this point in the sales funnel. They're not quite ready. Instead, they'll go looking for confirmation that this is the book for them. Reviews will be on the agenda. Or the preview. Likely both.

If we knew what they were going to do next, we could place a relevant CTA. We could say, *Look inside now.* Or *Check out the reviews.* There's nothing wrong with mini CTA's like this through sales copy. Amazon uses them in many places, including after the first few lines of the blurb where there's a *Read more* CTA that you click to read the remainder of the blurb.

But the key to effective mini CTA's is relevancy. Relevancy counts here, just as it does in all other aspects of marketing. You don't want to try to tell the prospect to read the preview when they want to read the reviews. Or vice versa.

The wrong CTA in the wrong place is annoying and counterproductive. You have to work with the sales funnel, not against it. Otherwise you're pushing water uphill. It can be done, but more likely you'll fall over in a muddy heap.

So, what to do? We end with the best teaser we can. This is a cliffhanger, and it drives the prospect to act just the same as a CTA. Better, actually. The only difference is that instead of us choosing the action, the prospect does. They want reviews? The teaser will drive them there. They want to read the opening chapter? The teaser will drive them there. The cliffhanger at the end has the psychological force to fuel whatever action they choose.

Skip back a bit and re-read the end of the last blurb. Quite a teaser, isn't it? And as much as I love marketing, that teaser is better than any version of "buy now".

By the way, I've read the book. Wilbur Smith delivers on that blurb. Big time. Check it out. But, you know, after you've finished *this* one please.

3. Seven Blurb Myths That Kill Sales

Are you still with me?

We've just covered some heavy material. The above was a snapshot of copywriting skills it's taken me many years to grasp. I don't expect you to take it all in at once. My advice, when time permits, is to reread it. Then Google the things I talk about. That will give you verification, but it will also deepen your understanding.

Time for something lighter. Let's do some myth-busting.

Myth 1: Blurb doctors

This is a term in high currency. Generally, it's applied to writers who help other writers with their blurbs on internet forums. They can gain quite a following, and their advice is soaked up by their followers and spread in turn.

The other type of blurb doctor is an editor. Some editors provide a blurb-writing service in addition to their normal editing function.

Some of these people give good advice. Others don't. If you don't have a copywriting skillset, it can be hard to tell the good from the bad. This means advice is taken on trust … and that's not a professional way to operate.

But can an actual, trained copywriter be a good blurb doctor? You may think this is a strange thing for me to say, but I think the answer is no.

A good copywriter can always write a tight blurb, full of hooks and structured according to AIDA or the sales funnel (they're really the same thing) but that's not enough.

The first rule of copywriting is to know your audience. The *golden* rule of copywriting is to know your audience. Everything arises from that. You have to understand them first. You need to be able to put yourself in their shoes, and think what they think and feel what they feel. You need to know the tropes of the stories they love. Otherwise, your copy won't resonate.

Can a copywriter do this? Of course. But only for some genres. I love epic fantasy. I understand the genre, and the subgenres within it. In a way, I live and breathe it. But thrillers? That's a different animal. Romance? A different beastie again. And so it goes.

Usain Bolt and Eliud Kipchoge are both runners. They're the best. But one's a sprinter and the other a marathon runner. I wouldn't expect them to swap places and run the other's race. Nor would I expect a copywriter to be able to write blurbs for all genres. Still less a writer or editor.

There's no such thing as a blurb doctor, and if someone gives advice on all genres (or worse, offers a paid service to write a blurb for all genres) then it sets off an alarm bell in my head.

Myth 2: Hooks are teasers

Most writers are familiar with the concept of a hook. A hook, as it's generally thought of, is some sort of teaser – something that poses a question that's only answered later. Whether it originated in literature or in the craft of copywriting doesn't really matter. It may surprise you to learn though that copywriting has been around since antiquity. The first sign hung over a tavern door in Uruk, Babylon or Antioch saying "tavern" was copywriting. The guy across the road who didn't have a sign for his own establishment … well, he watched all the hungry and thirsty travelers tramp down the road and go to the competition. He wanted them too, so he hung his own sign, this time in red and with a matching grape bunch. Something like that was the origin of copywriting, and marketing wars to boot.

Back to the point. In copywriting, a hook that teases and poses a question is called an open loop. It's a powerful tool. Extremely powerful. The experts say you have to start your blurb with one.

But an open loop is just *one* of many different types of hook. After all, the purpose of a hook is to attract attention and then drive people to keep reading. Why should a question be the only means of achieving that?

Here's another kind. I call it *The Statement*. It's popular in newspaper headlines (which serve as a hook to entice people to read the article), but it works for blurbs too. Here are a few examples.

Sir Winston Churchill Dead

Obama Sweeps to Historic Victory

Earthquake and Fire: San Francisco in Ruins

These were all real headlines. No open loops in sight. No questions. All that you really need to know is contained in the headline itself. But you can imagine the number of people who saw them when the things they described were fresh news, and went on to read the whole article.

Why?

Because the headline told them exactly what the article was all about. And they were interested in the topic. They read on for the specific details. This is what's happening in the Robert Ludlum tagline quoted above.

Here's another example. This is the start of the blurb from *Bury My Heart at Wounded Knee: An Indian History of the American West.*

The "fascinating" #1 New York Times bestseller that awakened the world to the destruction of American Indians in the nineteenth-century West (The Wall Street Journal).

Again, there's no open loop there. It tells us exactly what the book is about. What else is it doing? Well, social proof is a powerful hook as well. If other people really like something, we're psychologically primed to check it out for ourselves. The fact that the book was a *New York Times* bestseller is offering that social proof. So too the reference to *The Wall Street Journal.*

Here's another example. This one's from the opening of the blurb to James Patterson's *The First Lady.*

In James Patterson's new stand-alone thriller, one secret can bring down a government when the President's affair to remember becomes a nightmare he wishes he could forget.

Not only is there no open loop here, we get a downright spoiler. The President has had an affair. So, how do we deconstruct this one?

Firstly, the selling points. Just the name of James Patterson sells books. So that's frontloaded to the very beginning. I'm not sure that stand-alone is a selling point, but it's targeting an audience – those who like stand-alones in contrast to a series. It's also giving us genre-relevant information. *Thriller. Secret. Bring down a government. Affair.*

In its way, the statement is as powerful as the open loop. Perhaps even more powerful.

The moral of the story is that when you're writing a blurb, you have options. You want to start by attracting attention, but there are many, many techniques to do that. Pick the best one for the job out of all your choices. And if you can, get a few going at the same time. The best hooks are usually deceptively simple but multifaceted.

Myth 3: Blurbs must be written in third person, even for first person books

There used to be some truth to this one. Not now. It's a favorite among the blurb doctors, but someone better tell the bestselling indie authors in urban fantasy and romance that they're doing it wrong…

In some genres, first person is all the rage. Not so with others. As always, never take advice without verification. What are the bestselling authors in your genre doing?

First person has advantages. Remember we talked about emotion earlier? And how important it is in a blurb? First person allows you to connect just that little bit quicker than third. It's more intimate. Over the course of a whole story, I think this advantage diminishes. But in a blurb? Seconds count.

The key here, as always, is your target audience. What do they expect? What have they shown a liking for in the past? If they like first person, give it to them. If they like third, give that to them.

There's a bestselling author with at least one book that I know of where the story is in third person and the blurb in first. That's a total flip. But the book sold by the truckload. I mention this not to suggest you do the same, but to point out that readers don't know about "blurb rules" and nor would they care if they did. They just want a good story, and if the blurb hooks them, it hooks them.

Follow what works. Don't follow rules.

Myth 4: The blurb is set in the transition between act one and act two

Another favorite among some blurb doctors. They love their rules.

There's no doubt this is a good place to mine for blurb material. But, as always, dig deeper and seek out the truth.

Other places in the story are just as good. Sometimes, they might be better. As long as you're leading the reader through the sales funnel, interesting them and turning that interest into desire to read more, nothing else counts. If something from halfway through the book does this, or near the end, it doesn't matter. You can even give away a spoiler. You have more than *one* surprise in your novel, don't you? Just don't give away more than one. Or the ending.

To put it in marketing terms, a real estate agent doesn't show just the driveway and the front door to a potential buyer. They show them the whole house. But first impressions count. If they can, the agent will take their client to the best room first. They'll enter from the front, back or side door depending on which one best allows them to do so.

Not a perfect analogy. But the point is to use what works best, whichever part of the story it comes from. Constraining yourself to just one small segment is far too limiting.

I suggest you start at the start. Come up with the best, most attention-grabbing blurb opening you can. This will set up what comes next. If that happens to lead you into the second or third act, are you going to shred the blurb because someone on a forum said you're not allowed to do that?

Put your big boy or girl pants on, and decide for yourself what makes the best blurb.

This is an important aspect of what it takes to rise above standard advice and standard sales numbers. It applies to everything, not just blurbs. Dig deeper. Verify. Use what works. Find *best* practice; don't follow *accepted* practice.

For the record, lots of blurbs for bestselling books reach far beyond the act one and two transition. Not concrete evidence of best practice by itself, but an indicator.

Myth 5: Traditional publishers get interns to write blurbs

Maybe they do sometimes. And maybe the intern is good at it. Better that than a great editor who doesn't have the gift of writing enticing copy.

But when I look through blurbs for traditionally published books, I often recognize copywriting techniques in use. Maybe not always, and certainly I don't think a blurb is good *just* because it's for a traditionally published book. The establishment have their hits and misses like everyone else. Copywriters have hits and misses too.

Still, if we go back to the Robert Ludlum and Wilbur Smith blurbs above, they're dripping with copywriting techniques. No clueless intern wrote those. They were crafted by a pro. Possibly a team of pros.

The people who say you should ignore the blurbs of traditional publishers have their own books and courses to sell. They're trying to position themselves as the one true source of information. They make more money that way.

But the art and science of good blurb writing is free to study every time you pick up a book or browse Amazon. And if the blurb is no good, you can learn just as much from that as from a good one.

If you're going to study them though, here are a few tips to increase the chances of finding the best of the best.

First, look to the great authors. Wilbur Smith, for example, is a big-time author. Do you think his publishing house risks tens of millions of dollars, per book, by getting a rookie to write his blurbs? No. They put their best people on it. People with a history of writing blurbs for books that sold.

So what you're looking for are blurbs by bestselling authors, preferably with a large backlist of bestsellers behind them. They'll get the best treatment from the publisher.

The same applies to blurbs of indie authors – a good sales record over a long period of time. One book might be an accident. Or a BookBub featured deal. Multiple books that have all done well indicate skill.

Most of all, what you're looking for is a pattern across all these blurbs. Do they generally start with a big hook? Yeppers. Is that hook always an open loop? No.

And on it goes. Seek out the patterns. See how those patterns match copywriting techniques like a stencil laid over the top. When you see the same patterns, again and again in bestselling authors, and it matches known copywriting techniques, do you really think it's a coincidence?

It's no coincidence. It's genuine professionals at work. It's people who know copywriting. Learn from them. They're teaching you the skills for free.

The logic behind this one is simple. The theory goes that Amazon indexes blurbs, and if the blurb contains the keywords you want to rank for, then you'll get an advantage in search returns for that keyword.

Here's an example. Your novel is a coming of age fantasy. You insert coming of age fantasy somewhere in the blurb. Because you likely want to rank for epic fantasy and sword and sorcery as well, you do the same thing for them.

I've tried it. It made no difference. Amazon uses a hierarchy for these things, and keywords in the blurb are at the bottom of it. If at all. (The book title is far, far more important for this. More on that later).

None of this is a problem in itself. Except you now have a clumsy blurb that doesn't convert as well as it would. Oops! The quest for an advantage has delivered only a disadvantage.

Want to rank for a keyword? Make sure it's in your backend search terms. Put it in a few times and it'll enhance the effect. (Others disagree with this, but I've found it to be true). Of course, this comes at a cost. Whatever space you're using for that steals away from another potential keyword. Amazon only gives you so many characters in the keyword field. Use them wisely, grasshopper.

Also, you want to know the *best* way to attain rank for a keyword? Apart from having it in the title – which looks lame and is possibly a breach of Amazon's terms of service. Well, the best way to attain search rank is to sell well. This will place you *much* higher in search results. A bit of a vicious circle though, yes?

Here's something else to consider. It's estimated that seventy to ninety percent of sales come off Amazon product pages anyway rather than search results.

As always, dig deep and find the truth. Cheap tricks won't work. But they *can* backfire.

Myth 7: Don't reference other authors or books

Another blurb doctor favorite. Essentially, the advice goes that readers don't like it when an author compares themselves to another well-known author. For instance, a horror writer referencing Stephen King.

But the blurb doctors are either all in or all out. They love rules. There are no shades of gray, and most of all no understanding that in copywriting (as in most art forms) there aren't good or bad techniques – there's only good or bad execution of a technique.

In this case, a bad execution is to reference the other author or book in terms of quality. So a horror writer who references Stephen King that way is asking for trouble. Here's an example.

Love Stephen King's horror stories? This book is even scarier.

Now, it's possible the author *is* actually better at horror than Stephen King. But they can't expect the reader to believe that. And a prospect who doesn't believe what they're being told is a whole lot less likely to buy. Their defenses are triggered. This is, as the blurb doctors claim, setting the author up for failure.

How then can the technique be executed properly? Well, let's take the quality judgement out of it.

In the tradition of Stephen King.

What this does is inform the reader, more succinctly than any other possible method, what type of book they're looking at. It's not just a horror story (which covers a wide field) but a horror story in the style of the master. The prospect knows what they'll be getting if they buy it.

Remember I said in the previous chapter that the best way to get someone's attention was to give them what they want? Well, people love to read by genre. And when they find a favorite author, they're always on the lookout for books in the same vein. Stephen King is very popular, so this technique connects the wants of a vast readership to the book the blurb is selling.

This technique works. It can be even better though. It shines its brightest when there's a mashup of styles. The author could spend paragraphs trying to show what the world of their book is like in the blurb. Or they could do something like this.

Meet the Godfather of Sherwood Forest.

This is the cover tagline of the Robin Hood novel, *Outlaw* by Angus Donald. Just those few words give you a glimpse into the entire story. It's gold.

BookBub have researched this issue. Their split testing shows that referencing comparable titles results in an average increase in click-through rate of 25.7%.

That's a *stupendous* increase in click through. However, you have to be wary because that was on blurbs on their website (not Amazon) and the behavior of their specific audience may not perfectly reflect Amazon's wider audience. Still, it should give the blurb doctors pause for thought.

4. Covers and Eye-Tracking Technology

I've spent a lot of time on blurbs. This is because there are so many myths about them, and also because they're so important. But other factors are critical too.

The cover is one of those factors.

What's the purpose of a cover? And when I say cover, are you picturing a book in your hand? Or are you picturing a thumbnail image within a row of other thumbnail images?

You're probably thinking the first, but it's the second that sells the book. Recognizing this difference is essential to success. It's not easy, and you probably won't like it (neither do I) but it's the truth.

Picture that little thumbnail image, and then contemplate the golden rule of marketing, which is to think like the customer. Put yourself in their situation. How do they feel? What do they want? How will they know when they have it?

You'll probably spend several hundred dollars commissioning an artist for a cover. You might spend much more. But the prospect doesn't know that. Nor do they care. Nor should they. That's your problem, not theirs. They're just looking for a good read.

The prospect will glance at the cover for a second, maybe two or three, if you're lucky. That's it. So make it count.

Why is this so? Because when customers browse Amazon, they'll see your book cover as one image out of hundreds. If they spot it in a bestseller list, it will be just one of many. Perhaps they'll see it as an also-bought or as a sponsored product in the ad carousel. Wherever they see it, it will be just one drop of water in the ocean, one grain of sand on the shore. Click, and they're gone. That's all it takes. And it happens over and over again, all day long on Amazon.

Let's go back to the sales funnel. What's needed here is attention. Get that, get the customer's gaze to linger, and just maybe the next click won't be away but to your cover and onto your blurb.

And what's the best way to get attention? *The same as it is with blurbs.* Offer the prospect what they want.

This means that the cover should signal subgenre at a glance. Not just blown up (though it has to do that too) but at thumbnail size. If it's what the prospect is looking for, you have their attention. The cover beside it might be a better book, but if yours sends a clearer signal, it's the one that will get the click.

The image must resonate with genre. You can get a feel for this by picking an also-bought carousel. Flick through it quite quickly. Click, click, click – just like a prospect. See how long it takes to form an opinion about each thumbnail's genre. The answer is nanoseconds. Make your cover like the best of these. The ones that take longer than nanoseconds are the failures.

You might think that being also-boughts they'll all be the same genre. But you have to go deeper than that. You want to spot subgenre and mood. For instance, in epic fantasy, one book might be coming of age and the next assassin orientated, and then dragon based and … on and on.

Study the ones that jump out and tell you what they are quicker than your finger can click. What do they all have in common? This is going to vary by genre, so there are no hard and fast rules. Look for the pattern. It will probably be a simple design rather than a complex one. Simple works best in thumbnail.

What other signal should an effective cover send? Professionalism. It should look good. It should not look homemade. If the cover seems professional, the prospect will be more likely to think that the content of the book is good.

This is called the halo effect. It's a cognitive bias that if a person likes one aspect of something they'll be favorably disposed to think well of other aspects of the same thing, even if they're unrelated.

This is a bigtime marketing concept. It's huge. It doesn't just apply to covers, but to your blurb, preview and a bunch of other things as well. Each point of contact with the prospect is a kind of first impression. Make them all count.

The halo effect is a critical concept to grasp. I suggest you Google "halo effect in marketing". I have more to say on the subject in the minimum viable product chapter yet to come.

One other thing about covers. It's often stated that people are drawn to people. This is true. Cover artists (and others) will often argue that you must have a person on the cover, and preferably their face, because this will draw more buyers to it.

On the other hand, many people hate faces on the cover because they prefer to use their own imagination as to what a character looks like. They say putting a person on the cover could be detrimental to sales.

Who is right?

Remember I mentioned infrared eye-tracking technology earlier? It's a handy tool, for a bunch of reasons. On the subject of people's faces, the human gaze *is* drawn to them. No doubt about it.

For verification, Google something like "eye tracking web page" and then click the image tab. A picture is worth a thousand words.

I know that I suggest you verify things a lot. This is because I don't want you to take my word for anything. I don't want you to take *anyone's* word for anything. There's just no substitute for gathering the information yourself and making your own decisions. Following what other people say, even if they have the appearance of experts, is the best way to follow standard practice and to miss out on finding best practice.

Back to covers. So we've now proven that you're better off with a person on the cover. Yes?

No.

My other saying in this book is to dig deeper and find the truth. You really need to go into the detail of every aspect of the publishing business if you want to be successful. Either that, or get lucky. Both can work.

I place more reliance on digging deeper though. And what happens when we do so on this issue?

First, we need to make a distinction. Being drawn to look at a human face is one thing. Buying is another. The eye tracking confirms the first, but it gives no proof for the second. *None.*

In fact, some marketers claim that a face can alienate prospects. People are quick to judge, and they may not like the face. This takes us back to the halo effect, or the failure to induce it.

Other sources claim using faces increases conversion rates.

I suggest these searches to research the subject: "Why you should stop showing faces in your ads" and "do human faces on a landing page increase sales and conversions?".

After your research, take a deep breath. The evidence is mixed. And none of it applies to Amazon and specifically to how people buy books online.

So the jury is still out on this one. I don't know the answer, and I don't think anyone does. Not that people won't speak with great authority one way or the other.

So for the moment, I keep digging, trying to find the proof. And my fallback position until I discover it is to just keep doing what's common in bestsellers in my genre. For me, that could be a person or an object. Both work for epic fantasy. It may not be the same for you.

But remember, whatever genre you're in, keep digging for the truth. Don't accept the word of anyone about anything without verification. Even a cover designer. It's the searching out of best practice that will help you rise above your competition. It's work, but it's worth it.

5. The Types of Titles that Sell

Titles help sell books. In some ways, the title jumps out more quickly than the cover to a prospect searching Amazon (or any retailer). And it's capable of giving just as much information, if not more, in the briefest of glances.

For this reason, the title should be readable in thumbnail. If not, it serves no purpose being there. Worse, small and unreadable, it makes the image seem cluttered and unprofessional. This costs sales.

To achieve a readable title in thumbnail, you need a short one. But short titles make it difficult to convey information. Quite a dilemma.

By information, I mean words that will signal genre and that will attract attention. It's a tall order to do all this with a mere handful (actually less than a handful) of words.

But it can be done. At least, it can be attempted. And the more you practice, the better you get at it. It's a skill I was slow to pick up, but I've improved.

Here's something else to consider. The thumbnail image of the cover and the title are inseparable, and they operate as a unit. Not only does the title appear on the cover, but as text beside the cover on Amazon along with the star rating and number of reviews. This is another reason to keep it short.

Amazon only displays a limited number of characters, and titles are often broken off here. Make them short, and frontload something genre relevant or attention worthy. This mini text below the thumbnail forms part of the prospect's decision (along with the review information) on whether to click or not. Use every tool you have to attract attention and earn that click. The title is a powerful selling feature. It's an opportunity to let the prospect know the book is of interest to them. Don't let it slip by.

Of course, you *can* let it slip by. By itself, this is a small factor. Impact on sales will be real, but insignificant. This is not the attitude of a craftsperson at work though. You remember that earlier I said success was about getting all your ducks in a row? Well, this is one of those ducks. Any duck by itself is just a duck. Get a bunch together, and you have a flock. And a flock of ducks, wheeling and turning in the sky in mind-boggling synchronicity, is an awesome sight.

So, to summarize, keep titles short so they're visible at thumbnail. Pick words that signal genre. Frontload them to the beginning so the text next to the thumbnail helps you sell.

That's about it.

But as always, if you dig deeper you find more. We've only just begun.

Some titles can invoke a sense of mystery, or gravitas, or comedy, or emotion. All powerful tools, and all useful if chosen to match the genre. And just like the tagline of a blurb, using multiple techniques will get you better results than one alone.

Also, titles and covers are at their best when they work together to reinforce a concept. So keep your mind open when thinking of a title as to what a cover artist might be able to do to reflect the title in the imagery they use.

Showing is often better than telling, so here are a few examples of good titles and my deconstruction of them.

Tomorrow, When the War Began

This is an old favorite of mine. The title is a type of hook which I term "the say whaaat?" It's more common in advertising. Sometimes you see it in blurbs. Using it in a book title is fairly unique, but also quite powerful.

It operates by subverting reality or expectations, and therefore causes startlement. This is what gains attention. As you can see, it's more proof that hooks are far more varied and complex than the superficial advice that they're teasers posing some sort of question.

The "say whaaat?" can be incredibly powerful, but its effects are short-lived. All hooks are short-lived. Many only operate for a few seconds because the human mind is always jumping around thinking of something else.

If you want longer lasting hooks, you have to base them in emotion. But for a title, or a blurb, the "say whaaat" is awesomeness incarnate.

I'm Fine and Neither Are You

Wow. Here we go again. I said the "say whaaat" was fairly unique, but even so you start to see it everywhere once you recognize it for what it is. Copywriting. Not random chance or accident, but design. Those people who say traditional publishers are clueless about this sort of thing are wrong. Publishers (often) know what they're doing. Study them and run what you see through a copywriting filter. You'll see the patterns emerge.

I spoke above about how the title and the cover can work together to offer a unified concept. This is an example. There's a kind of antithesis between the two halves of the title. This is reflected in the two heads on the cover, one facing up and the other down.

The Atlantis Gene

This is a nice, short title. It pops incredibly well on the cover. It also does a fairly good job of conveying genre, which is mystery and suspense. These type of thrillers tend to have very similar titles. If it's not jumping out at you as such, it might be that you're not familiar with the genre. To me, they all have a similar feel to them, just as literary titles have their own unique feel.

It's not easy to do much with three words, but that title does enough and it visually pops.

Love in Lingerie

Again, it's not easy to say much in three words. This title manages pretty darn well though.

But if you see it on Amazon (to help you find it, the author is Alessandra Torre) you'll see how the cover image and the title are working in unison. And not just the title, but the *font* of the title. There's also some clever (and suggestive) design work going on with a zipper. Everything is working together. More on the concept of continuity later. Suffice to say, it works.

Warning! It's Billionaire Romance. Don't look if the image of two people getting hot and heavy is off-putting to you.

Melt

Okay. You looked for the previous book. I know you did.

For those few who didn't, here's an entirely different (and much tamer) example of the same thing, only this time the genre is post-apocalyptic. The authors are JJ Pike and Mike Kraus.

Again, it's a short title that pops on the cover. Its presentation (font, color and design) work in unison with the cover imagery to signal genre.

This is by the same authors, and the same comments apply. But it's book two of the series (the third is *Bury*) and it's an example of cover branding across a series.

See how the titles are in the same vein? And the imagery of the covers and the color palette? Not to mention the position of the author names and the fonts? Everything is working together to give a sense of sameness.

This is branding. Prospects who have read book one and then see book two will recognize it when they do. If they're going click, click, click through an also-bought carousel this will jump out at them.

The important thing here is that the covers look similar so they can be recognized, but not so similar that they can be mistaken for each other. You don't want the prospect to take other books in the series for the one they've already read.

6. How Continuity Fuels the Sales Engine

So far, we've discussed the blurb, title and cover. This is basically the digital package in which a book is wrapped and presented to prospects.

Reviews are part of the package too, but I leave them out as they're largely out of your control. If you have an advanced reader copy (ARC) team from your subscription list, you have a little more control. But given that you're giving a book away for free to fans so that you can get (probably) favorable reviews (because they're fans) you have to wonder if Amazon will crack down on the practice at some point. I'm not sure how they would do that, but you can bet it's something they've considered. The review system is broken, and they've taken drastic steps in the past to try to make it more transparent and organic.

The last part of the package is the preview. I'm not going to discuss that much here either, because what goes into the preview falls more to the craft side of publishing than the business side.

But not entirely.

The preview forms part of the basis on which a prospect makes their buy or don't buy decision. No marketer or business owner would ignore ways to lever that.

I've talked about the sales funnel in this book. Imagine trying to pour gas from a gas can direct into a mower fuel tank. It would splash all over the place. No matter how careful you were, a lot of it would get wasted. That's why you use a funnel.

A sales funnel works the same way. It captures a wide flow of prospects and directs them to the end of the spout, which is a buy button on Amazon (or the fuel tank in your mower).

Now imagine filling the mower tank again. This time you're using a funnel, but it has holes in it. You pour the gas through, and what happens? Some goes in the tank, but you've still made a mess. Gas has leaked.

The same thing can happen with a sales funnel. You can leak prospects, and the main reason for this is a lack of continuity.

The title, cover, blurb and preview should all be on point like synchronized swimmers at the Olympics. They should work together to sell the book, and they do this by giving the prospect the same message.

If something is out of step, the prospect begins to get confused. Maybe the book isn't of the type they thought it was.

And confused prospects don't buy.

Please don't underestimate this. It's critical. But as always, verify for yourself. Google something like "confusion kills conversions". You'll see what I mean.

Let's look at a hypothetical book example. But hypothetical or not, it's the kind of thing you see over and over again on Amazon.

Let's call our imaginary book *Sword of the Barbarian*. To me, that gives off the vibe of an old-school sword and sorcery story. Conan himself would be at home in a book like that.

That title will attract the attention of a certain target audience. But what if the font for the title is in a style more commonly used for thrillers? A little bit of confusion creeps in.

What's on the cover? Let's put a young boy there, his hand outstretched and some sort of magic light emanating from his palm. Now the prospect is starting to think it's a coming of age fantasy story.

Next comes the blurb. This tells us that the boy's parents have been killed. He's an outcast from his village and hunted. Already his best friends have died to protect him, except for the one who betrayed him by revealing that he has secret powers and can command fire. But, if he can reach the witch in the wood, he might escape his enemies yet. And there he might learn magic, and one day return as an adult to bring vengeance to those who destroyed his life.

Well, now things look pretty glum. This seems to be dark fantasy.

Then we go to the preview. What awaits us there? A prologue set in ancient days describing the origin of the kingdom and how magic was banished, but that it would rise again when the Skull King returned to try to conquer the land once more.

Oh my! That's epic fantasy, and I love it. But the prospect has been through the dishwasher. They don't really know what kind of book this is going to turn out to be, and they now have strong doubts that it's the old-school sword and sorcery that they were initially hoping for.

Click. They're gone. Despite all these genres being in the same ballpark as each other. Close enough often isn't good enough.

But if the cover, blurb and preview all matched the vibe of the old-school sword and sorcery title? Cha-ching. You have a sale.

There's great power in continuity. It's a wave that brings people along for the ride, becoming ever more gnarly as it gathers itself together.

Let's look at it from a different angle. How good is the movie *Jaws*? Can you imagine it though without the iconic music? How powerful that music is! How well it works with the images on the screen to ratchet up the tension.

It's the same with *The Terminator* theme music. Or food. It doesn't taste so good if you can't see it. Or smell it. And the list goes endlessly on.

There's power in continuity. Learn how to harness it in creating the book "package" and it'll serve you well. Fail to do so, and your sales funnel will leak.

7. The Secrets in Plain Sight

I touched on this concept when I spoke about Amazon not putting a buy CTA at the end of a blurb. It would be easy for them to do so, but they don't. Instead, they put it at the end of the preview. Or, if the prospect decides to buy before they get to the end of the preview, there's one on the preview's left panel.

It's reasonable to deduce this indicates that most prospects read the preview, but not everyone reads the *entire* sample. Probably, the first page or two is enough to reassure most people that the desire built up by the blurb isn't misleading. Either way, Amazon have it covered. There's no need to click back to the product page. They make buying convenient. More evidence that a buy CTA at the end of the blurb is misplaced.

Amazon's tactics on these matters are plain for all the world to see, but how many authors notice? How many ask why?

Well, we will.

This is the thing we have to train ourselves to do all the time. Asking questions is the key to success. Why is there a CTA here, but not there? Why is the buy button orange? Why is the buy button on the left of the preview page and viewer browsing history and also-boughts on the right?

The more you train yourself to do this, the better you understand the Amazon ecosystem. And because the website is designed to mirror buyer behavior (as all good websites are), the better you'll understand how to market to Amazon customers.

There's a critical nugget of information there. It bears repeating. *The website mirrors buyer behavior.* All marketers and webpage designers strive to understand buyer behavior patterns and design their sales funnels and page layouts to optimize customer satisfaction (and therefore sales). The placement of CTA's is a massive clue to buyer behavior.

Here are my answers to the questions I posed a moment ago.

The orange color of the buy tab is irrelevant to authors. But as a side note, most buy buttons are colored blue because blue is shown in testing to be the most liked and trusted color. Likewise, red signifies danger. You'll rarely see a red buy button for this reason. So why do Amazon use orange? Because it's their brand color, and by using it for a buy button they're associating themselves with a feeling of trust. Blue would have worked better initially, but now people know they're well-covered by Amazon's policies for refunds etc. They have trust in them. And they've learned to *trust* that orange buy button. Now, whenever they see an email promotion or anything else from Amazon with their distinctive orange colors, they're more likely to trust it at a glance. This means more sales.

As for the buy button being on the left panel of the preview page, this is because it has higher visibility there. Google "F-shaped reading pattern" for verification. Look at the infrared eye-tracking images. Amazon puts the most important stuff here because they want a sale. The stuff in the right panel is less important (or, if you prefer, less used by customers) so it's in a less visible situation. But it must still be important, otherwise it wouldn't be there at all.

Interestingly, if you click out of the preview page you see this situation is reversed. On the product page, you click the cover to get to the preview, and the cover is on the left. The buy button is on the right. This indicates that on the product page, Amazon know more people want to click through to the preview than to buy. But once inside the preview, client behavior changes. That's when they want to buy, so the buy button is moved to greater prominence on the left.

The important concept I'm trying to convey here is that we're not privy to Amazon's marketing meetings or the thinking of authors on the Top 100 list. And yet nearly everything they do is visible to us if only we take the time to look and ask, "why have they done that?"

The Top 100 list is fruitful territory for this. Some industry advisers dismiss popular authors. They claim the author may have gotten there by luck. Or they may be succeeding despite doing things the wrong way. Or they haven't split test blurbs, so they don't know what works and what doesn't.

This is a critical error. Or, the adviser knows better but is deliberately trying to position themselves as the sole source of reliable information. They probably have a course or something to sell, and they want you to rely on them.

My view is that not everybody on the bestseller lists knows what they're dong. But many of them do. It's insulting to suggest otherwise. They've reached that point through hard work, and a better understanding of marketing than others. They often come from a non-writing career that positioned them well (like me) to understand the *publishing* aspect of this business. And they network with other successful authors to share tips and strategies.

Study them. But don't form views based off what one of them does. Look for the patterns across multiple successful authors. Verify the techniques and strategies they use against proven marketing methods. This is the way to dig deeper and begin to find best practice.

Best practice is rarely revealed in an internet forum. But it's there, plain to see on Amazon, if only you look.

So, what are a few things you can learn by looking at the Top 100 list?

I find this interesting. Looking at the Top 100 Paid for Fantasy in the Kindle Store (as at March 2019) every single item is a kindle book. No surprise there.

But, let's look at the Top 100 Paid for Fantasy in the Book Store. Here, I count fifty-three audiobooks and forty-seven kindle books. There isn't a *single* paperback or hardback. It's a somewhat similar situation in other categories.

Why?

That's always the question to ask. The top of the page tells us that the listing is based off the most popular products. Fair enough. If that's correct, it tells us that ebooks and audiobooks are selling a *lot* better than paperbacks. But something else is also evident. Shoppers can only buy what they see…

In the Kindle Store, they *only* see kindle editions. That's it. But in the Book Store, Amazon is happy to mix things up. Kindle editions, audiobooks and paperbacks all jostle around together. But there are still only 100 spots, and this limits the potential sales of physical books. It can't be clicked and bought if it isn't visible. Every kindle edition or audiobook on that list is suppressing visibility for a paperback that would otherwise be there.

So, Amazon appears to be *deliberately* pushing kindle books at the expense of physical books.

There's another indicator of this. The F-shaped reading pattern shows browser behavior will focus on the left of the page. Therefore, the left is likely to sell more than the right. When we look at a kindle product page, the various editions of the book are listed in a horizontal line close to the top of the page just below the title. And the kindle edition is placed first on the left.

But what do we see on a paperback product page? The kindle edition is *still* listed first on the left. It has extra eyeballs on it. This is Amazon's way of giving it additional push.

There's a war going on between Amazon and the Big Five traditional publishers. It's covert these days, unlike a few years ago when the US Government filed a suit on the basis that Apple Inc. and the Big Five publishers conspired to illegally raise and fix the price of ebooks sold on Amazon. The publishers settled, but Apple went to court. And lost, ending up having to pay $450 million.

It's a cold war now. And Amazon is silently winning it. The pushing of one product and the suppression of its rival over a long period will eventually cause change. Bit by bit and increment by increment, like a glacier moving down a mountain one pace a year.

All this is a glimpse into the future, and it'll be one dominated by ebooks. At least on Amazon, and that's where most people buy. This is good for indies.

Back to our more immediate concerns. Any page on Amazon is an excellent place to study and ask why they've done things a certain way, and what we can learn about buyer behavior from it. Remember, we don't have statistics from Amazon, but they do. The way they organize their pages reflects what they know about their customers' behavior.

Let's have a look at the product page of an ebook. Note, these comments are based off viewing on a notebook computer. A smartphone is a little different. For space reasons, I'm only doing one analysis here.

In prime position we have an image of the book on the left, and the book title top and center. These are both occupying critical real estate. Both will get viewed. Michael

Alvear has commissioned some infrared eye-tracking tests of this, and I suggest you study his heat map. (Google Michael Alvear eye-tracking). The results are exactly in line with general research of eye-tracking on any webpage.

Essentially, both cover and title get looked at. Below the title is important information such as author name, and a snapshot graph of the number of reviews and the star rating. As well as the price. All this gets a lot of eyeballs, for obvious reasons.

The prospect has now gained considerable data about the book in a very short period. Amazon frontloads what's important to customers instead of making them click for more.

Then comes the blurb. Critically, Amazon only provides the first portion here. Why? I believe that most people won't read all of it. Amazon used to provide the lot, but their statistics probably showed that the majority of people weren't reading to the end. So, being customer-centric, they ditched it in favor of a blurb snippet and a CTA to click *if* the prospect wants to read more.

The lesson here? Make sure your blurb opening attracts attention and then interest. Fancy tricks like using HTML coding to display large fonts won't do you much good. If anything, it's harming those who use it. Use bold or italics though, if you want. Customers are habituated to this, and it draws the gaze. But most of all, make sure the opening sentences signal the *content* of the blurb is interesting. Frontload a hook in just the same way Amazon frontloads what they know customers want to see. If you give the prospect what they're interested in, you're a better chance of them clicking the "Read more" prompt at the end of the blurb snippet.

There's no way to know what most people do next. Do they click away, finish the blurb, click "Look inside" or go down the page to the also-boughts or reviews. We just don't have the data. But my deduction is that if the blurb beginning doesn't work, many, many people look down at the also-bought carousel. We already know this is a powerful selling tool, and Michael Alvear's infrared testing appears to confirm it.

But what else can we deduce from clues in the way Amazon structure the webpage? The blurb comes before the full review section. This indicates prospects want to read the blurb *before* they move to the reviews. And given the preview is still in sight and clickable at the end of the blurb, but the reviews require a lot of scrolling to reach, I think more people go to the preview than the reviews.

As a separate issue, also-boughts come before the sponsored product carousel, at least when they're shown toward the top of the page these days. This indicates that also-boughts are more used and trusted by prospects. But Amazon makes the sponsored product carousel look so similar to the also-bought carousel that the difference is probably only minor.

I could keep analyzing the product page, but those are the main things that concern us at the moment.

Next, let's turn to the Top 100 Bestseller List in the Kindle Store. This is where you'll see the most successful authors. What secrets are visible in plain sight here?

First, the books are numbered from 1 to 100, in Amazon orange. This is part of their branding process. But much more relevant is this – the covers are *all* good. Every one of them. There are no shockers there as you sometimes see in lesser lists. Note, liking or disliking a cover and it being good or bad are not the same thing. One is about personal preference and the other fitness for the function it performs.

Look at how many short, but big and bold titles there are. This sells books. Making them resonate with genre sells even more.

The covers are the dominant feature of all that you see on the page. Study them and see the pattern of what makes good ones.

But the covers aren't *all* that's there. There's very little space with so many things jumbled together in rows, so you can bet Amazon puts there only the things that sell books, or that at least get a click to somewhere else that may sell a book.

The title sits below the cover. People will look at it even though they saw it on the cover. This time, they'll also see at least part of the subtitle that probably isn't readable on the cover. Make your words count. Note also that the title is clickable. Confirmation that people read and click it. Note as well that the click takes them to the blurb.

The author name is there too. This offers brand recognition. People want to read authors they've read and liked before more than anyone else. Click the author name though, and you're taken to the author's page on Amazon rather than the blurb.

Why?

Amazon wants to sell the book, so shouldn't they send the prospect to the blurb and product page?

I can't repeat this enough. *Amazon is client-centric.* They organize their website to suit client behavior. That the link takes the prospect to the author page means people want to go there. Amazon works *with* their clients, not against them. The lesson here is for us to do the same. Make your product page sing. But make your author page sing too. Customers want to view it.

And what's on the author page? Your books, sortable by format. Your biography. A list of also-bought authors (rather than also-bought books). These are all factors that influence a prospect's decision to buy or not. And there's a "follow the author" button too. The link wouldn't take prospects here if they didn't use this page. We have control over portions of it, so make it good. Don't focus on the product page alone as the selling tool.

Back to the Bestseller List. Below the author name comes the star rating and number of reviews. Again, I emphasize that this must help sell books, otherwise Amazon wouldn't put it there. Sell is the wrong word. It gets the prospect's *attention*. Click on this part, and it takes you to the full review section. Again, not to the blurb.

What does all this prove? Amazon knows their customer's purchase habits. And those habits are variable. Amazon works with the customer, and we should too. Don't get into a fixed way of thinking. Make all parts of the sales funnel sing. At least those parts you control.

Something else is interesting. The price is usually included below the star rating, but not always. You know what's coming.

Why?

When included, the price links to the blurb. But why isn't it *always* included? That it's usually there indicates it's important to customers (duh, that's a no-brainer) so why not all the time?

As it turns out, most of the time it's not there the book is traditionally published and has a much higher price. Is this another tactic in Amazon's war against the big publishers? I can't see any other explanation. Whatever the reason, its effect is to skew sales towards indies (because displaying the price assists the prospect's decision-making process).

The last thing I'm going to note about the Bestseller List is that embedded within it are links to two other lists. These are the New Release List and the Movers and Shakers List. Again, these links wouldn't be here if those lists didn't sell books. But they don't sell as many as the Bestseller List, otherwise the Bestseller List would be embedded into them instead. There's a web-design hierarchy to these things.

Time to click on a Top 100 bestseller. Any one of them will do. Now we get into the really useful stuff. These are authors at the height of success. They may not broadcast their tactics on blog posts or internet sites, but whatever they do is in plain view if you only look.

We've already discussed blurbs, so I'm not going to offer further comments on that here. Pricing strategies and writing in a series are obvious tactics we already know. But *how* long should a series be? Looking at the tactics on display, the sweet spot seems to be between five and ten books. Why? Because the more books in a series the more you can bid in advertising. But there comes a point where readers want a resolution to the story line. And a new series is a new entry point for readers and another book one to advertise. Length also comes into it if the author is in Kindle Unlimited.

The lesson here? Most bestselling authors are packaging their stories in a way that maximizes advertising potential and sales, but minimizes reader dropout over a long series. Marketing over art? A good or a bad thing? You decide. But it *works*. Don't write too short. Don't write too long. Maximize entry points into your writing.

Time to turn to the also-boughts. What do they tell us? Well, they have a clear message, if you look. People who buy indie authors tend to buy other indie authors. Conversely, people who buy traditionally published books tend to buy other traditionally published books.

What can we deduce from that? That within the Amazon store there are two separate market streams. Indie and traditional. So, be careful of following trends in literature, because those trends might be all the rage in one market but not the other. Here's an example. Traditionally published epic fantasy has a history of doorstoppers. That trend continues. But it's *not* the same for indies. Here, there are authors making a living releasing books less than two hundred pages. Most are between two hundred and three hundred. Rarely are they six hundred. The lesson? Like any good copywriter, a good author knows their target market. Study what works for indie authors, especially when that's different from what traditional publishing is doing. Recognize where the two markets overlap and where they diverge.

Time for the Sponsored Product carousel. Can we learn bestselling author strategies from what's in view there? You bet we can.

Bestselling authors aren't just advertising book one. They tend to advertise several books within a series. This is obvious at a glance from the carousel. Conclusion? It's working for them or they wouldn't be doing it. It's not cheap to advertise on a Top 100 book.

Let's turn to their sales copy in the ad. First of all, using that mini sales copy at the bottom of the ad is optional in the US store. Are they even using it? Yes, they are. Why? Probably because their testing shows it works better than the option for no sales copy.

There's a lot to learn from those mini blurbs, but most of it falls outside the scope of this book. But this much is important to note. A lot of them mention "free in KU". Many of them aren't plot based. Instead, they talk to the reader directly, which is a big sin according to blurb doctors. They say things like "Do you like XYZ heroines who do ZYX? Well, here she is…"

Some of these authors are keyword stuffing in the ad. There's a valid reason for it here (as opposed to the normal blurb). More about that in the Amazon ad chapter.

There's more to learn. This is by no means uniform, but there's a distinct trend for books on the first page of the carousel to have more reviews than later pages.

Why?

The first page is prime real estate as it gets more eyeballs on it. Is it that authors who sell well get more reviews and can therefore bid higher? Probably that's part of it. But Amazon also tells us in their help pages that bid price is only *one* factor that determines ad placement. More on this in the Amazon ad chapter, but I believe reviews are playing a part in ad placement. They don't impact sales rank, but they're an indicator of popularity and Amazon always want to put the books that sell in front of buyers in preference to books that don't sell as well.

Have you learned a few things here? I think even veteran indies will have been surprised once or twice in the last few pages.

The key to it all is to look and learn. Train yourself to stop and ask *why*. Study the secrets in plain sight, and spot the patterns. Then test them yourself to see if the tactics work for your specific genre and books. But most of all, keep digging. Keep looking for that gold. Stop following standard advice and try to catch the wave of cutting-edge practice. That's the way forward.

8. How the Pros Write to Market

Whether or not to write to market is an issue that has fried the servers of every internet forum where writers gather.

Writing to market has been put on a pedestal. It's been knocked down. It's been celebrated as the cornerstone of success. And it's been compared to selling your soul to the devil.

There's lots of views out there about it. But let me say two things…

Firstly, you don't have to write to market if you don't want to. Art is art, and you need pay no attention to anything but your muse to create it. To hell with anyone who claims otherwise.

Secondly, if you want to *sell* your art, it pays to pay attention (a lot of attention) to marketing considerations such as what people like to buy.

The choice is yours, and I'm not about to tell you what to do. But, if you do want to write to market, here are a few tips.

Most write-to-market advice starts like this. Find yourself a niche that seems to have reasonable reader demand, but one that's not too competitive. That's where opportunity lies.

Stop right there. That advice seems to make sense. It's logical. It's certainly the standard advice. But it's deeply flawed.

If you follow standard advice, you'll get standard results.

The best you can possibly expect from this flawed method is to succeed at becoming a big fish in a small pond. And probably only for a short while as others spot the same opportunity and publish in the niche until market saturation occurs.

I think there's a better way. If you want real success, the sort that enables you to write for a living, you need to move into a bigger pond. You need to swim with the sharks and not the shark-bait.

But *can* you move from one pond into another? Your mailing list is a critical tool. It'll probably be useless to you if you swap genre, even subgenre. Readers generally don't follow. Not in large enough numbers.

And this is another factor. What it takes to succeed in any genre, but especially the competitive ones, is a deep understanding of readers at a subgenre level. You need to live it and breathe it. You need to know what readers like and don't like, at a *microscopic* level.

The only way to get that is to write, publish, read and study that subgenre and its authors. Swimming in the smaller pond doesn't teach you this. So, when you move to the big pond, you're starting from scratch.

It's a far, far better strategy (and I say strategy rather than tactic because this is a long-term approach) to pick one of the super-competitive subgenres for which you have a passion. *Start* there. Build up your knowledge. Build your mailing list. Work your way up by increments.

In the long term, this is the shortcut to success. This is where the money is.

There's something else going on here too. Writing full-time, hitting bestseller lists and competing with the big dogs is about skill and knowledge, but it's also about attitude and confidence. You have to back yourself. No one else will. No one else will do the work for you. No one else will plan the best strategies for your author brand.

You're in it by yourself. You'll stand or fall by your own actions and choices. And it takes guts to do that. It takes boldness.

But you know how the saying goes. Fortune favors the bold.

So, do you back yourself? Are you willing to do the hard work? Are you bold enough to dive into the big pond? That's where the pros swim. That's where true opportunity lies. That's where long-term financial rewards await.

9. Why Great Books Fail

I know you've seen it.

A book rises high on the Amazon charts, and conquers everything before it. You see it everywhere. It's on bestsellers lists. You spot it in ads. The cover stares at you from a Goodreads page. Soon, you begin to wonder if the damn thing is going to turn up in your pocket when you're looking for small change.

Finally, you get the time to click on it and have a look. The blurb seems okay. You check out the reviews. A whole bunch of them have gathered faster than seagulls fighting over spilled fries. Most of them say the book is pretty good. The reviewers that is, not the seagulls.

But this isn't your first rodeo. You know a lot of those reviews are from the author's ARC team. Of course they're good. So you click on the three-star iterations, and read them. They're probably left by organic readers.

You don't learn much though. No major faults with editing. No big plot holes. Some people just liked it more than others.

What next, grasshopper? You scroll back up and click "Look inside." You know from past experience that the only definitive way to see how good the book is … is to read it. Or at least the first page or so. That's usually enough to discover how well it resonates.

So you do that. And nothing jumps out at you as being particularly bad. But nothing seems particularly great either. It's ordinary.

You scratch your head. Why is this book hot property? Why is it topping the charts? It's not bad, but you've read a hundred like it that were just as good. Only they never achieved liftoff and orbit on Amazon. What makes this book different?

You click to the author page to see if you can learn something there.

The author is a newbie. You see they published the book two months ago, and it was their first. Holy hole in a donut Batman. How is it possible?

When you get over your shock, you see they've also been prolific. Books two and three have since been published and book four is about to drop.

Stop right there.

Do you believe well-written books succeed and poorly written ones fail? Do you believe the cream always rises to the top?

Or do you believe that good marketing is what counts? If an author masters that, then they can promote dross to the top of the store?

Or, do you believe in luck?

I'll tell you what I believe. I'd as soon try to convince Tom Cruise that Scientology is whacko than pay what it took to promote a dud book. And I certainly believe in luck because I've had my share. But I believe more in getting all my ducks in a row so that when Lady Luck chooses to sashay past, I'm ready to give her a roguish grin and try my chances.

I know this too. There are plenty of good writers out there. Plenty. Many of them don't sell well. They plod away, working all day at the regular job, finally clocking off to commute home and then cook dinner. Eventually, feeling like an exhausted zombie coming down with zombie-flu, they force themselves to write for half an hour before their body gives out on them. Then they crash into bed, dreaming of doing it all again tomorrow. Or if they're luckier, chocolate-frosted donuts.

I know because I used to be one of them.

They probably publish one book a year. Maybe one every two years. The first book in the series may have got off to a promising start, but sales died months before book two was near ready. And when book two finally lands, crickets. The author begins to wonder if their skill has deserted them. Or maybe they had a bad cover. Or possibly the blurb was no good.

Poor sales could be for any of those reasons. But it probably wasn't the cause. Just as in life, timing in publishing is everything. And for everything that happens, there's a reason. If you don't know what that reason is, you call it luck. If you do, you call it good planning.

Back to the author page we were looking at. We can see that multiple books were published in short succession. Could this be the reason an ordinary book achieved Amazon stardom?

You bet it is. At least, probably. The author likely had a lot of ducks in a row as well. Maybe nothing stood out as brilliant, but at least everything they had was acceptable.

The one thing in this business that works better than anything else is a rapid-release strategy. It's sometimes called the Liliana Nirvana technique. You can Google that for verification and further research.

The problem with the rapid-release strategy is that it requires multiple books ready for release at pretty much the same time. Most authors can't write that quick. I'm a fulltime author, but it takes me at least three months to write a novel. To have three ready requires over nine months without a release. This is venturing into dangerous territory. When you write for a living, it's nice to publish books regularly in order to, well, have a regular income. Still, it *is* possible.

But if a fulltime author struggles to pull it off, it's much harder for a part-time author.

Or is it?

I suggest, if you're trying to break into this business, you build up those three novels (all in the one series) before you release. No matter how long that takes you.

So why does the rapid-release strategy work?

First of all, it's not guaranteed to work. Nothing is. But it pumps up your chances for success like a bodybuilder pumps up steroid-enhanced muscles.

This is how it's generally supposed to function. There are cliffs on Amazon. The thirty, sixty, and ninety-day dates of doom. Most authors experience a decline in sales at those points.

Why?

Because Amazon (despite what some people will tell you) does a lot to promote your book for free. For the first thirty days a book appears on the New Release lists for its categories. We talked about this earlier in passing. These lists are important, otherwise Amazon wouldn't embed them into the Bestseller Lists. People use them. Avid readers scour them, seeking out fresh material to read. Those lists sell books.

On top of this, Amazon gives a new book extra juice in search results. If you've written a book involving shapeshifting unicorns, and shapeshifting unicorns is one of your metadata keywords, Amazon lifts it higher in the search results for anyone who searches that term. This extra juice dries up after a month.

When your book is a month old, it drops off the New Release lists and loses some of its visibility. Sales consequently decline. Not to mention interest is probably starting to decline among readers anyway – your biggest fans have already seen it and bought it. Sales can still be good, but they dwindle of their own accord as a separate thing to dropping off the New Release lists.

Thus the cliff. The better your book launches, the more that cliff is a gradual decline. The worse your book has performed, the steeper the drop off in sales.

We won't go into the second and third cliff. It's pretty much the same explanation.

But, so the rapid-release theory goes, if you publish book two in the series a month after the first, then you have another book in the New Release lists. It has the visibility book one is losing, and it picks book one up, gives it a pep talk, and gets it to perform again. In turn, book three does the same to books one and two combined a month later.

You've tripled your visibility by quick releasing. You've doubled it timewise on the New Release lists. Hey presto, this is a big advantage over the guy who is still sitting on book one only and seeing sales deflate with no real hope of changing the situation because book two is still six months away.

Does any of this reflect on the quality of the books or the relative skill of rapid-release authors versus slow-release authors?

No. Not a bit.

One author is utilizing a marketing technique that the other isn't, that's all.

This technique was discovered by accident in the early days of indie publishing. Indie publishing arrived, and some authors had bunches of manuscripts hidden away on their computers. They released them quickly, and the magic began to work. There are quite a lot of millionaire authors walking around today because they stumbled onto the technique.

Is that all there is to the strategy though? Is that really how it works? I've never seen a deeper explanation than that. But, I think I can add another layer to it. More than a layer. This, I think, is the secret sauce that *really* serves up success.

To explain what I mean, we first have to go back to the sales funnel I talked about earlier. Only this time think a little bigger. Go beyond title, cover, blurb and preview to how prospects actually flow through the funnel in terms of sales numbers.

Let's look at that bigger picture, but how it plays out in three separate release scenarios.

Scenario one

This is a stream of buyers over a period of time. They each read book one. Then they finish, and there's no book two. Book two is scheduled for publication six months down the track.

As is usual, some readers didn't like book one. They've crossed you off their list. They'll never buy book two. The rest is divided into two groups. Those who loved book one desperately, and those who thought it was okay, and they'd be willing to read book two when it came out.

Unfortunately, most people are going to be in that second group. How many authors have you read that were the bomb compared to those who were okay? Most of us only rarely find an author we truly love.

What happens over the intervening six months? Some of these readers will have stopped reading or switched genres. Most will have read dozens of other books. Probably all but your small number of die-hard fans will have forgotten you even exist.

You release book two … to crickets. Few people buy it. Amazon's algorithms note the low sales figures and decline to promote it. It descends rapidly into the primordial ooze at the bottom of Amazon's digital shelves.

Sure, you can promote book one at the time you release book two. This may give it the breath of life. But probably not.

Scenario two

You release book one and two on the same day. Of those who read book one, most go straight on to book two. Your sales funnel is working perfectly, or at least as good as can be expected. No one has a perfect read-through rate.

Your backmatter from book one is propelling them through. Amazon is pushing you. You're on the gravy train. Book two will have a very similar sales rank to book one.

This could be the same book one and book two as discussed in scenario one. The quality of the writing is the same. The spend on advertising is the same. The readers are the same. But the release strategy is different, and it gives much, much better results.

Over and above everything else, you're getting the benefit of visibility from two books at the same time. This lifts your sales. So, in effect, book one does better than it would have if released by itself. And because the readers are immediately funneled to book two, you're on a double-decker gravy train. To be honest, I don't know what a gravy train is, still less a double-decker one, but I'm sure you take my point.

Scenario 3

Now, imagine book one is released, and book two followed it two weeks later. That flow of readers from book one to book two can't quite happen. They'll know book two is coming very, very soon though (because you wisely told them so in the backmatter of book one). So they wait on it, and they don't forget because they don't have time to forget. It's only two weeks.

Then you publish. In scenario two, let's say you averaged twenty people a day buying book two. Now, you have a similar number of people, but multiplied by fourteen days. That's two hundred and eighty people.

Big difference, yes? Now, they may not all discover the new book or buy it on the same day. Let's say they buy it over five days. That's fifty-six sales a day. But you still have the daily flow through from book one to two, which is twenty a day. That's a total of seventy-six a day.

Jackpot. The sales rank of book two will spike massively. Its visibility on bestseller lists will climb sky high. That will lead to a whole bunch more people seeing it, and going back to buy book one. And Amazon's recommendation algorithms will get a nice little tickle under the chin, waking them up and setting them to action.

Book one, that used to sell twenty a day, may now sell thirty or more a day, and start feeding those extra buyers to book two.

Then, of course, two weeks later you release book three. Shazam! The cycle commences anew, but even stronger.

See now why rapid releasing is such a good tactic? Do you see now why books no better (or worse) than many others propel their authors up the charts and into indie nirvana?

I've no doubt about this tactic. It works. The reason above in scenario three is why, though I don't believe anyone else has ever stated this publicly before. Everyone talks about the cliffs. They're part of it, but not the main reason for the tactic's success. It's the bottleneck of buyers coming though in a steady rush that lifts the sales rank and stimulates the algorithms.

The only question I have is how to time it right. I've done simultaneous releases. I'm experimenting with scenario three right now. But maybe waiting one month between releases is better than two weeks? Or maybe not. More experimentation is needed here. More pooling together of results. It's a lot easier to succeed as a group of people sharing knowledge than as one alone. I'm working on that too. More later.

Anyway, there you have it. It's one of the main reasons (probably by far the biggest) that some authors get ahead and others equally as good, if not better, don't.

If ever a technique existed to push maximum results with minimal skill and effort, it's this one. Add skill and effort to the process, and you're as close as you can get to guaranteeing success. Not millionaire success like the goldrush days of indie publishing, but still blow-your-socks-off success. Take it if you can get it.

If you remember, I said in the introduction that it wasn't enough to work hard. You also have to direct your efforts with correct knowledge. After reading this last tactic, do you agree with me?

10. Minimum Viable Product Theory Debunked

The concept of a minimum viable product goes like this. A business (in this case a publisher) releases a product (in this case a book) with just enough features to satisfy early-uptake customers (in this case readers).

There are benefits to this approach. First and foremost, it's cheap. In book terms, there are no fancy covers required. A cheap one will do, even a fifty buck pre-made. Editing is done on the cheap too, if at all. The book may only get a look-over by a fellow writer or the like.

The real point of it all is to test the waters. Instead of assuming there's a market for a particular subgenre, or that a mailing list will follow an author if they swap genres, or that a particular style or voice or trope subversion will resonate with readers, the author tests for it.

As I say, the book is published on the cheap, and it's probably short too. It's put out there to see how it goes and to get feedback in the form of reviews.

Then the author is in a position to see if it's worth their while to ramp up production in that series. If so, better covers will follow. More will be spent on advertising and editing. The books might be longer, and better written.

So far so good. It can certainly be expensive to publish. A good cover might be $600.00. Editing a similar figure, or more. Advertising. Well, how long is a piece of string?

Publishing can be expensive, and this test model approach cuts right back on that. The whole model was popularized by a Silicon Valley entrepreneur called Steve Blank and another entrepreneur called Eric Ries.

This is one of the things Mr. Blank had to say about it. "You're selling the vision and delivering the minimum feature set to visionaries, not everyone."

Therein lies the problem. Despite how popular this concept is becoming in the publishing world, it was never meant for books.

Are readers visionaries? Perhaps some of them are. But mostly they read in their tried and trusted genres that conform to the standard tropes. Authors might play with those tropes, but for the most part they keep them.

If an author wanted to use the approach as it was intended, then it might work for something like a new genre mashup. Say, billionaire bad boy meets epic fantasy.

So far as I know, that's never been done before. I doubt it would work, but you never know. Enter the minimum viable product. The author can suck it and see, so to speak. If it takes off, they can ramp up production, release a better quality follow up, and ignite a whole new genre, or at least trend.

But is that how it's being used in publishing? Very rarely. Mostly people use the concept as a justification to release on the cheap. The very cheap.

I understand the expenses involved in publishing, and I'm all for finding the cheapest way to do things. So long as everything still remains fit for purpose.

The great danger of the minimum viable product approach is that the author publishes material that isn't quite good enough to resonate with an audience. This will have a two-fold effect. Firstly, sales won't be good. But even more importantly, you only get one chance to make a first impression with a reader. If they find your offering, and judge it not up to scratch, your job of convincing them to buy at some future point in time is much, much harder.

No thousand-dollar cover in the future, nor thousand-dollar editing job is going to remove that lingering doubt they have about you. *You've damaged your brand.* You might win them over eventually, but probably only some of them.

So, if you use the concept of minimum viable product, I suggest you use it as intended – for something truly new and unique. And probably under a pen name.

If, on the other hand, you're releasing into an established subgenre, try your hardest to have every aspect of your release competitive. Otherwise, how do you expect to *compete*? You're setting yourself up for failure before you begin.

Get it right the first time, if you can. And better still, follow it up with books two and three in short succession. This is the opposite of the minimum viable product method, and it'll serve you better.

11. The Science of Purchase Psychology

Let me ask you a question. Do you think it's a good idea to try to build a car if you don't know how an internal combustion engine works?

Few would try. And fewer still would succeed.

Marketing is no different. Without the skillset, you have as much chance of doing it effectively as the person trying to build the car. But the skillset can be learned. If you want to succeed on a commercial level, you're going to want to think about investing the time to do so.

That's the bad news. The good news is that it's not really that hard. You just need a primer in the basics. You don't need a doctorate in it.

And the basic concept of marketing is the sales funnel. Once you grasp this, everything else will follow. It's the key concept. Everything stems from it.

Why?

Because the sales funnel has nothing to do with you. Or your wants. It has nothing to do with your preconceptions or personal preferences. It's about the customer. It's all about them, and how they think.

In a nutshell, that's what good marketing is. Putting yourself in the viewpoint of the customer. If you do that, you're light years ahead of everybody. Because most people don't. Even many industry figures. It's all about them, and what they like and react to. Their opinions shape their marketing, and this leads to bad decisions.

Flip it. Put the customer first. Empathize with them.

There's another way of looking at this. Most people would say marketing is selling something to someone. Nope. No way. The best definition of marketing is that you bring a person's attention to a product they *want* to buy. This is the internal combustion engine of marketing.

If you understand the differences in those two approaches, you're on your way to becoming a marketing guru. Namaste, grasshopper.

Once you reach that understanding, there's a whole field of scientific research that helps you put yourself in the customer's shoes. You can then anticipate what they want, and give them that when and how they need it.

The psychology of the sales funnel

We talked about AIDA and the sales funnel before. They're more or less the same thing. The sales funnel is a recognition of the psychological mindset of a prospect at different stages during the course of a buy/don't buy decision. AIDA is a formula for copywriters to prompt them to do certain things as those stages progress.

This is the sales funnel again:

Awareness of the product
Evaluation of the product
Interest is stimulated
Interest transforms into desire
Action occurs (buy or don't buy)

Awareness of a product is where it all starts. You can't buy what you don't know is for sale. This is where Amazon, BookBub and Facebook ads come in. Or newsletter promotions. Or an Amazon Countdown deal. These are all tactics to promote awareness.

At this stage of the process, a prospect's defenses are up. Everyone wants a buck from them. People lie to them all day long. On the news, all they hear is spin from politicians. In short, they're skeptical. And they have a right to be.

But if you can get their eyeballs on your product, you've made the first step toward a sale. The second step, the one that makes them click on a cover, or read more than the first line of the blurb, goes a little beyond awareness. It requires that you signal that what follows is of interest to them.

The best open loop (hook) in the world can't do this by itself. No matter how intriguing, interest is never really generated. Curiosity is, but curiosity is fleeting.

Here's an example:

Read this and you're guaranteed to live to 110.

Scientists have discovered that a healthy diet and exercise is the key to longevity. And there's nothing healthier to eat than avocadoes. Here, at Avocado Farm, we produce great...

The first line is an open loop. It's so open you could fly a plane through it. I'm sure that would generate a high concentration of eyeballs.

But it's also clickbait. What gets your initial awareness is never delivered in what follows. You feel cheated. Probably for the hundredth time today.

Have we learned something here?

Treat your prospects with respect. Lure them in, by all means. But then deliver the goods. It's the congruency between how you begin and how you follow through that sells. Awareness is the foundation, but you can't build on it if the ground is shifting quicksand.

The prospect's psychology here is one of skepticism. Get their attention. Then start to build trust. Throw as large a net as you can in marketing to get as many eyeballs as possible on your product. But start by selectively *targeting* those prospects. Put yourselves in their shoes first. Don't advertise to them if they're not interested in what you have. Respect them, and don't waste their time. Then, once you have the maximum attention, begin to deliver.

This takes us to the evaluation stage. This is a continuum, and it's hard to say where evaluation turns to interest that in turn becomes desire. It happens progressively, but not necessarily the same way for everyone. We all have different triggers. For instance, price might drive some, but not others.

But marketers know what fuels this stage. It's your job to provide it. This is done by building interest, by stoking it like they used to feed coal to the steam engine of a train.

Another way to look at it is this. What information does the prospect need to evaluate the product? They want price. They want to know if it's value for money. They want social proof that others have tried and tested the product – and liked it. Most of all, they want a feel for the product itself.

Give them these things. Don't hold back. Give them the same information you would want in their place. Trust their judgement. Don't try to *convince* them to buy. That's spin, and they're sick of it. Their defenses will never come down that way. Instead, connect them to a product that you think they'll want to buy. If you have to try to talk them into it, your targeting was out in the awareness stage.

If you do this, the prospect will give you their time and evaluate what you're offering. Interest will grow. At a certain point, it might become desire.

This is where we turn to the action part of the funnel. At this point, it's about making it as easy as possible to buy. They should know exactly what to do, and that action should be easy. For instance, Amazon has it down pat with the "buy with 1-click" CTA. The prospect's psychological state at this point is that they want to buy. The CTA tells them exactly how to and makes it super easy for them.

What follows are a few of the core tenets of behavioral economics and marketing, and my comments as to where and how they apply in the sales funnel. Academic studies and split testing have proven them, so they're worth their weight in gold (or at least in book sales).

Behavioral economics

Homo economicus: It's a play on words, but it's also an important concept. The rationale is that people as a generality make choices based on self-interest applied through a filter of rational and stable preferences. In order to "nudge" people in a desired direction, you should appeal to them via logical data to convince them.

Behavioral economics challenged this traditional economic theory, and won. People often *don't* make the rational choice. No amount of "convincing" them will convince them at all. You have to appeal to a deeper level of the human mind. You have to go beyond rational thought and into emotion.

This concept is important in blurbs, but it's important in backmatter and newsletters to clients too. When you want someone to do something, it helps to give them a reason. Often, a logical reason isn't enough. For instance, you can offer notification of future discounts as a reason to sign up for a newsletter. It's logical that if someone liked your book, it's a good idea for them to sign up. But this tactic is ineffective. A possible discount at an indeterminate point in the future carries little weight. Nor does it trigger an emotional response.

Backmatter, blurbs, author bios and newsletters are all specialized areas of sales copy. There are ways to trigger emotion (even for a newsletter signup) but there's no room in a general book such as this to discuss them. They require an entire book themselves in order to do justice to the subject. Stay tuned, that book is coming.

Rules of thumb: Surprisingly, people make 95% of their choices on rules of thumb. These are mental shortcuts that spare people from having to think. Thinking takes a toll on the body (seriously) because the brain is the most energy-demanding organ of them all. It prefers to cruise along in idle rather than put the foot down on the accelerator. This is a concept of critical significance to things such as cover design in the hectic digital world where people have smaller attention spans than goldfish.

You may have heard a good cover stands out. Nope. People apply rules of thumb to a cover to make a snap decision of click or not click. Does it signal genre? Yes. Does it look professional? Yes. Rule of thumb? The book is of a kind the reader might like. Click.

If the cover is quite different from what they expect, they have to analyze it to try to form an opinion. This requires effort. Effort is work, so many people will pass it by looking for easier choices.

The rule of thumb concept goes deeper than covers. It has wide-ranging applications. Most of them come to the fore in situations where time is limited and quick decisions are necessary. Think BookBub ads and the like. Here, limited information such as the number and general rating of reviews and the price enable snap decisions. This can be quite different from, say, a prospect leisurely reading the preview. To nudge people at these different stages within the sales funnel requires an understanding of their different mindsets at those points in time.

Cognitive biases: These are fascinating. Briefly, they're a little like the rules of thumb we talked about before. But rules of thumb tend to be consciously learned behaviors. Biases tend not to be. People, if asked, can explain their rules of thumb. But biases operate under the radar, even of the person displaying them. Anchoring is one. The person will rely heavily on one piece of information, which is usually the first they have. This has ramifications for blurbs in particular, and taglines especially. They can "shape" how the entire blurb is perceived.

The bandwagon effect: This is also interesting. It's a tendency to believe things that other people believe. Social proof (such as review quotes in blurbs) harness this bias.

Hyperbolic discounting: This is useful to understand as well. Essentially, people prefer more immediate payoffs than later ones. This can be very important when you're trying to get someone to do something. It's one of the reasons a free book in exchange for an email address works well as an incentive. There's an immediate payoff as opposed to just signing up to an author's list to hear about future releases. Not that I'm necessarily recommending this. I'm just giving one of the reasons it works. It has drawbacks too.

Salience bias: This is yet another bias (out of a great many). How this works is that a person is more likely to focus on something that stands out. Sounds obvious, doesn't it? It can be sneaky though. Writing the price of something in a small font can nudge someone to perceive it as a "lower" price, and vice versa.

This kind of thing can backfire badly though. Write a price too small, and people realize you're trying to trick them. This is bad marketing. It's also why the giant font at the top of some blurbs comes across as gimmicky. It's trying too hard, and prospects get wary. Applying it to covers, it might sound like it counters the rule of thumb concept discussed above. But getting attention is one thing, and decision-making afterward is another.

Marketing psychology

Marketing shouldn't feel like marketing: This is a key concept. The moment a prospect senses they're being manipulated, their shields go up. Likewise, the moment you try to manipulate someone, that's the moment you shift from good marketing to bad marketing. Your fundamental aim as a marketer is to connect someone to a product that they *want*. Remember this, and it'll serve you well, no matter if you're writing a blurb or trying to determine the target audience of pay-per-click advertising. Don't try to change people's minds. Don't lie to them or deceive them. Offer them something they want at a fair price. Do that, and they'll keep coming back for more.

Marketing is an experiment: For all the science behind marketing, no one has done an academic study of your product and your target market. You have to take the general concepts and apply them to your own unique situation and with your own unique style. Don't be afraid to experiment. Don't be afraid to get it wrong. All marketers, no matter how good they are, get it wrong at first. But the good marketers use any results, good or bad, as feedback and prompts to improve their next marketing iteration. It's a process of refinement. The tortoise always wins this race. Never the hare.

Emotion appeals to buyers more than benefits: People don't read fiction for information. They read it for enjoyment. People don't even read nonfiction for information (unless they have to). They read it to make their lives better in some way. Or because they enjoy learning the information.

Less is more: Enough said.

Create scarcity: This ties in with your author brand. Write like you, and no one else. If a buyer can buy your book from someone else, they don't need you. If they like your style, and can't get it elsewhere, you have a seller's market.

What's in it for me? This is what the prospect is always thinking. It's what we think when we're prospects in our turn. If you want someone to do something, and you don't know what's in it for them, or there's *nothing* in it for them, you have a problem.

Use a call to action: CTA's work. But put them in the right place. In the wrong place, not only do they fail to achieve their purpose, but they draw attention to the fact you're being manipulative. That's not going to end well.

There you have it. The briefest of snapshots into some important marketing concepts. A drop in the ocean, really. But have you noticed something? Although behavioral economics and marketing approach things from different angles, they come up with similar answers.

Remember that I keep harping on about looking for patterns? This is what you want to see. And not just in theory like we've been discussing here, but in practice in the marketplace. Look for the patterns on the bestseller lists, and you'll find them. Look for the techniques discussed above, and you'll find them all through the bestseller lists. It's no accident. The people at the top, or rising to the top, know stuff.

You can study marketing for a lifetime, employ it professionally and still turn up valuable insights every day. This is why I get grouchy at some industry "gurus" who publish marketing books and charge high fees for entry into their courses when they know little more (and sometimes less) than the people paying.

As usual, it's a case of buyer beware. There's always someone looking to make a buck off you. This applies especially to indie authors.

12. What Amazon Ads do that Other Ads Can't

Don't get me wrong. I have nothing against BookBub or Facebook ads. For that matter, I have nothing against the newsletter promo services either. They can all be useful.

But useful is a vague term.

You know my motto now. Dig deep and find the truth. Don't accept standard advice – seek best practice.

The truth is that each of these platforms gives different results. And I don't just mean sales number results.

Is one buy the same as any other buy? Does it make a difference to anything, anywhere, anyhow if the sale comes off BookBub or Facebook and *not* Amazon?

Turns out it does.

As always, you have to go back to the buyer and what they do. When you think only from your own perspective as a publisher, you miss things.

A 99-cent promo deal clicked via BookBub is going to yield the identical royalty as an Amazon ad on the same book. But the BookBub buyer is coming from the BookBub platform. If they click the buy button on your book, you get a buy. And that's it.

If the buyer, however, is browsing Amazon, you get not just a buy but a *conversion*. This has important ramifications.

Let's say the buyer is a fan of *The Da Vinci Code*. You write thrillers, and you're trialing a Sponsored Product ad on that famous book. The buyer sees your ad, clicks, evaluates and ends up purchasing your book. You've now converted a sale off *The Da Vinci Code*. And Amazon's tireless algorithms know it. They store that data away.

You keep that ad running because it's working for you. Next thing you know you have a second conversion. And then a third.

The algorithms prick their cute little digital ears. They're like a dog scenting out a trail. And there *is* a trail. Your book is being clicked on and converting off another book, and this indicates *relevance*. People are looking at *The Da Vinci Code* because they like a certain type of thriller. Your book is similar enough that people like it as well, and start to buy.

On Amazon, about 80% of products are sold off another product's page rather than via the search bar. (As always, Google for verification). If you're converting off a product, Amazon knows it and they want your product in its ads instead of a product that *isn't* converting. They make money from clicks whether they convert into a sale or not, but they make *more* money if the click does result in a sale. Not to mention, relevant books in ads makes for a better shopper experience. And Amazon likes to keep their customers happy. Happy customers now translates into more sales in the future.

Have you ever wondered how people can afford the bids on Amazon ads needed to hit the front page of a Sponsored Product carousel on a bestselling book with a stellar sales rank?

Well, they're not paying quite as much as you think. Relevance counts. It counts big time. And clicks and conversions build relevance.

Some people say that bid price is what determines ad placement. They go on to say that if you're crazy enough to pay astronomical prices per click, that will get you to the front of the carousel too.

This is dead wrong. Amazon even tells us it's dead wrong. They're quite specific in their help pages that bid price is only *one* factor in ad placement. Relevance is another. They don't reveal how their algorithm calculates it. But advertisers know the biggest factors are clicks and conversions. Other things probably come into play too (such as metadata) but to a far lesser extent.

Another way to put this is that your ad has a relevance score. This is consistent with other pay-per-click advertising platforms such as Google and Facebook. The relevance score is used to help determine ad position.

Low click and non-converting ads have to have higher bids to get to the front of the carousel. High click and high-converting ads need lower bids for the same, or better, placement.

This makes it easier to afford that first page of the carousel, even the first spot on it. If you get clicks and convert, you're paying less.

You can probably hit it with just high bids too. But if you don't convert profitably there, you'll soon switch that ad off. It's a money sink. If you don't, Amazon will. They'll shuffle other books into the spot that *will* convert.

So far, so good. You can benefit from this if you target your ads well. Targeting means ditching keywords that are less likely to convert in favor of those that are more likely to convert. This is a no-brainer, really. Why would you want to target less relevant keywords for lower conversion rates? It's not a good practice for a range of reasons. More on that later.

But this is all fairly passive. Is there a way to harness this knowledge to drive even better results?

Yes there is.

It's called seeding. You can actively grow relevance by advertising a book on a free or 99-cent promo via Amazon ads on highly targeted products. Free and 99 cents generate a high number of clicks and convert much better than full price, so you can build relevance against those keywords.

This comes at an upfront and immediate loss. Free and 99 cents don't earn much. But in exchange, you get months, even years, of higher relevance against those targets and consequently lower costs per click and better ad placement. This will often recoup your outlay quickly, and then drive long-term profits. Just be sure to target well. If you don't, poor click and conversion rates will erode your gains after the promo is finished.

There you have it. BookBub and Facebook ads (or any non-Amazon ad) just can't do that. So, I suggest you use Amazon ads more heavily than the other options.

But the other platforms have their uses too. And powerful ones. For instance, BookBub ads are responsive. You can turn them on or off like a tap, and once you get the hang of them you can generate a lot of sales in short order, which is pretty handy for book launches.

So, as always, it's not a case of which tactic is better. It's a case of which tactic to use at a given time and how to execute it properly.

Knowledge, as they say, is power.

13. Amazon Ads: How Real Gurus Make Money

Amazon ads attract as many myths as blurbs do. Believing these myths is what costs people money and stops them reaching their sales potential. No matter how hard you labor, your efforts are likely to prove futile unless that work is guided by correct knowledge.

A good understanding of how Amazon ads work is important. Amazon is a pay-to-play platform. As time progresses though, and the market becomes even more competitive, knowledge of how to successfully run ads will become far more than important – it will become critical.

Myth 1: ads die

Ads don't die. But Amazon *does* kill them. There's a subtle variation of wording between those two statements, but a profound difference in a practical sense.

I've had good ads run for years. I've torched bad ads after a week or so. And therein lies the difference. The quality of the ad is what drives its longevity. A well-targeted ad, properly supported by an adequate budget, bids and established relevancy, can last a long, long time.

Depending on how well the book sells, and how hard you advertise it, conversions might begin to fade after several months. Or years. This is because the pool of buyers on Amazon isn't limitless. But for most genres, you have to sell a *lot* of books to reach a point where the ad becomes stale.

The myth that ads die has a logic along these lines. Ads only last a short period, so delete them and start again. Seek out as many keywords as you possibly can. Keep repeating the process. Bid extremely low, and if you get an ad that actually seems to gain a few impressions, raise the bids by 2 cents periodically.

The problem with this theory (at least the main one of several) is that it never seeks to figure out why ads die. It just assumes that it's the natural state of affairs. But if you keep trying to alleviate the symptoms of the disease, rather than the cause of the disease, you'll never find the cure.

What happens is this. Amazon is pretty fair-minded. They'll give a new book a go. Or a new ad. If it performs, the algorithms notice and begin to promote it. If it doesn't, they shunt it to the back of the queue.

An ad will often accrue impressions for a few days when it's activated. Amazon is giving it a chance. But if those impressions don't lead to a reasonable click-through rate (an indicator of relevancy and customer interest in the product) Amazon will kill it. It's a non-performer.

Kill is probably too strong a word. Stifle is better. They'll still run the ad, but impressions will drop off and with them any real chance of conversions.

The remedy for this situation is *not* to make more bad ads and enjoy a few days of activity while Amazon trials it. The remedy is to learn to make relevant ads that get clicked, which in turn makes Amazon want to keep them alive.

Keep this at the front of your mind. If the ad doesn't get many clicks, Amazon doesn't get paid much. If the ad doesn't get many clicks, then Amazon customers aren't being shown a product they have interest in. If the ad doesn't get many clicks, you, as the advertiser, have little chance to get conversions. In a low-click scenario, everyone loses. What possible reason would Amazon have to perpetuate this? Especially when there are advertisers out there who understand the game and play by the rules. They submit ads that perform.

Myth 2: Use as many keywords as possible

This is closely related to myth 1. People are told this is the way to scale. The more keywords you have running (and by more, I mean thousands to tens of thousands) the more you sell.

This is *not* true. Not only does it not work, it has a negative impact. Those energetic Amazon algorithms track everything you do, and if everything is telling them you don't know how to run ads, Amazon is less and less inclined to want to show your ads. And more and more inclined to charge you a higher price if they do show them.

And lots of keywords with a bad click-through rate (CTR) tell Amazon that customers don't like your ads.

What you need are as many keywords as you can get that are *relevant*. For most books this is probably well under one thousand.

Sure, you can pay to put an ad for a book about alien time-traveling unicorns on an Agatha Christie page. You might even jag a sale or two. But it's not a long-term plan. That's not where your buyers are hanging out. Your CTR will be low, and your conversions with it. This sends a message to Amazon that your ads stink in the same way that blue dye in a pool reveals a peeing kid. You don't want Amazon to see you as that kid…

Myth 3: Amazon's suggested bids are far too high

This is a fascinating topic. The bottom line is that I don't want you to bid high. I don't want you to underbid either. I want you to bid at the level that brings you the most benefit.

That bidding level is controlled by the price of your book, whether or not you write in a series, how big that series is, buy-through and read-through rates and your conversion rate. These are all controlled in turn by other factors.

The good news? *All* of this is under your control. Some things, like price, you can change instantly. The number of books you have, and how you package them, that takes a lot longer. But it's still under your control.

So, never bid more than you can afford. But do you think it would be prudent to try to position yourself so that you can bid high, low or medium as *you* choose?

Putting aside what you can personally afford to bid, this is what happens on the Amazon ad platform in general. A person can bid 25 cents when the suggested bid is 70 cents. But they'll get virtually no impressions. They can then raise bids by 2 cent increments. It's a tactic, but it's the long, slow, boring way to advertising death.

The truth is that if the suggested bid is 70 cents, this reflects what a lot of authors are actually paying. You probably need to start bidding a few cents *above* that mark to start seeing adequate impressions.

Don't believe me? I don't blame you. A lot of people have been taught the low-bid myth, and what I'm saying here is hard to swallow. But if you're following the low-bid advice, is it working for you? Are you getting lots of impressions? Are you getting clicks off those impressions? Are those clicks converting? Do your ads perform for months and even years? Most of all, have you been able to scale up to commercially significant levels?

If not, try to keep an open mind about what I'm saying. You only get what you pay for, and if you pay in bananas you get monkeys. But don't take my word for it. Bid low and see how many impressions you get. Then bid high and see how many impressions you get. The statistics don't lie.

And you need impressions to get clicks, just like you need clicks to get conversions. Bidding too low is like putting water in your car instead of gas. It doesn't ignite, and you go nowhere.

The real problem is not how *much* you have to bid to get results, but how much you can *afford* to bid. This takes us back to the chapter on the secrets in plain sight. Look at the people advertising on books with expensive bids such as those on the Top 100 list. How can they afford it? Or are they all idiots who don't know what they're doing, and bidding month after month unprofitably? Some advisers would have you believe that.

But it's not true. These authors follow a clear and obvious strategy (if you only spend the time to look). First, they seed their relevance as discussed above. Second, they advertise boxed sets and books belonging to a long series. Third, they have a good read-through rate from book one and onwards. Fourth, they have a good conversion rate. They've positioned themselves so they can afford to bid high.

You don't have to do this. Not at all. Especially if you're happy with the odd sale here and there from an ad. But commercial-scale success needs more than the odd sale. People looking for commercial-scale success position themselves for it so they can bid above the suggested bid level, and get those impressions, clicks and conversions.

None of this should be taken as advice to bid higher than you can afford. The idea is to learn the tactics that enable you to bid high and *still* afford it, should you choose to do so. That's what will keep you competitive.

Two things to note. If you're bidding high, see where this lands you on the ad carousel. If you're landing first, you can reduce the bid. You might still be first. Play around (up or down) until you find a bid price and ad placement that you're happy with. Secondly, the actual average cost per click is sometimes 30% lower than the bid. So a bid of $1.00 might only cost 70 cents per click. That's a huge difference. But you have to test this. Sometimes the cost per click will be very near the bid.

If $1.00 seems a high bid, bear in mind that some of your competition could be bidding closer to $2.00. They can do this because the package they're selling (box set or series) is bigger. Package size really does matter.

All the above applies to fiction. Nonfiction is a slightly different animal. It's nowhere near as competitive as some fiction genres. You can still get impressions at reasonably low bids. So next time you're on a forum and someone says they're bidding low and getting sales, ask if it's nonfiction. And if they say it's fiction, ask them how many extra sales the ads are generating. One extra sale a fortnight isn't going to achieve much, no matter that they're doing it at a profit.

I know the true believers in the low bid philosophy will have read everything I just said, and dismissed it. All I ask is that if you have to bid low to bid affordably, please don't assume everybody thinks and acts the same way. Your competition isn't. They've taken the steps needed to ensure they can bid higher than they used to, and they're ahead in the race. If you want to run them down, you'll need to change the way you operate.

On the subject of Amazon's suggested bid prices, there are many who say they inflate them in order to make money. This is given as a reason why you should bid low.

Does this theory hold up? Let's compare it to Amazon's model of doing business elsewhere. If you read a fair bit, KU is dead cheap. If you buy ebooks, they're dead cheap too. Paperbacks? The same. Any product in the store? It's the same again. Amazon does everything they can to push prices down to get high volumes of consumers. That's their business model. Frequent purchases with a lower profit margin earn more than infrequent purchases at a higher margin.

Why wouldn't they do the same with ads? They want the highest possible uptake of ad users. They'll make more money from this in the long run than charging fewer more. Higher suggested bids are nothing to do with Amazon, and everything to do with authors positioning themselves for advantage against their competition.

Myth 4: Amazon's reporting is inaccurate

There used to be some truth to this. But not much. Amazon didn't report KU page reads against an ad. This was most annoying. However, there was a pretty reliable workaround.

But sales? Seriously? Do people really believe that a company that delivers books to your door by drone don't know when someone clicks your ad and then buys one of your books? Of course they do. And they report it accurately, otherwise they face fines and the prospect of their directors shuffling around the corridors of the big house in orange suits. I know Amazon like orange, but I'm pretty sure they're not that fond of it.

But that doesn't mean they report data straightaway. Ad data and real-time sales are never going to align at the same time. The attribution window for a sale off an ad is fourteen days. You can't expect the two data sets to match up at the same time.

But if a keyword says you've had five sales off it, then you've had five sales off it. You might have had more that aren't showing yet, but they will. Give things a bit of time, tally up the page reads, and you have an accurate means of measuring ad performance.

I mentioned above that there was a simple workaround for page reads. This isn't redundant. It still comes in handy when you start ads the first time on a book, and therefore don't have any ad data yet from sales and page reads. You do want to estimate what they might be, though, in order to arrive at a ball-park figure for what to bid. This is because how much you expect to earn influences how much you bid.

All you do is calculate your average ratio of full page reads to buys from your KDP dashboard. This can vary a lot on a day-by-day basis. It can vary somewhat on a week-by-week basis. But not really by that much.

The ratio varies by author and genre, but one sale to two borrows (full page reads) is common. If that's your ratio, then for every sale you have that's worth X amount in royalty, you average two borrows that are a worth Y amount in royalty.

I should mention at this point, despite Amazon now reporting both sales and page reads, there are one or two ad "gurus" who still advise ignoring ad data and just attributing *all* sales and page reads to your ads. This method takes no account of organic sales. At all. And for many, perhaps most authors, it will result in funding dud ads that are losing money.

Is it a coincidence that some of the main proponents of measuring total ad spend against total profit have a book or course on Amazon ads to sell? Is it a coincidence that some of these same people also promote the myth of inaccurate reporting? It's reasonable to ask yourself if it's in their *interest* that you think reporting is inaccurate and that ads are profitable (even though you might be losing money on them but still making a profit off organic sales). If you think these things, are you more likely to believe your money was well spent, and recommend these "gurus" to other people so they can sell more books and more tuition?

Cynical questions, I know. But the Romans had it right: *homo homini lupus*. A man is a wolf to another man.

Picture yourself justifying whatever method of measuring ad effectiveness you choose to an accountant. Ask yourself the questions you think the accountant would ask you. That might give you clarity.

There you have it. These are the main myths. Once again, I urge you not to take my word or another adviser's word for anything. Use your own common sense. And do your own research.

Now, time to turn to a more positive note. What follows is a brief guide on how to advertise on Amazon successfully. It's what I do, and it's part of the reason I'm able to earn my living at this writer gig.

Step 1

Have a good product to sell. Marketing can only connect someone to a product. It can't *make* them buy it. If you're not converting well, you need to look at your price, title, cover, blurb and the book itself.

Step 2

Tie your products together in a box set or long series. Make sure the writing at the ends of your stories drive readers through to the next book. Make sure the copywriting in the backmatter reinforces this.

Step 3

Find as many *relevant* keywords as you can. These are the ones that will best convert. It's not enough to target genre to genre. You need subgenre to subgenre. This is a *minimum*. Even at the subgenre level different authors have different styles and moods. Only some of these will convert well for your own style and mood. This is the place to experiment. Small things can make a difference here. Does your blurb show a female main character? It will probably convert better against books that do the same. This is the kind of thing you're looking for. Layers of similarity beyond genre and subgenre. Keep keywords that convert. Turn off keywords that don't.

Step 4

This is a doozy. Remember that I said earlier in this book that there are markets within markets? And that Amazon and the Big Five publishers are in the middle of a cold war? Well, this step takes that war into account. It stops you from getting friendly fire.

Generally speaking, people who buy traditionally published books buy mostly traditionally published books. People who buy indie books buy mostly indie books. People who buy paperbacks buy mostly paperbacks. People who buy ebooks buy mostly ebooks. Obviously, there's crossover. But we're looking at the main trends here.

What does this mean for Amazon ads? What does it mean for targeting and conversions?

It means that if you're an indie and you target a popular author within your subgenre by author name or book title (which is the generally advised thing to do) your ebook will show in ads on either ebooks or paperbacks, probably both, and *all* at Amazon's discretion.

But buyers browsing Amazon's Book Store are not (on the whole) looking for ebooks. If they were, they'd be browsing in the Kindle Store.

Roughly half the impressions you get in such a scenario are dead impressions. You were never much chance of getting a sale. Certainly not no chance, but a greatly reduced chance.

Why does Amazon do this? Why do they show your ebook ad on paperback books? Is it because they're trying to lure paperback buyers away from traditionally published books and to the Kindle Store? You think you're advertising your ebook, but in reality, is Amazon using your money to advertise the Kindle Store to paperback buyers?

Not nice, but there you have it. Something in the vicinity of 50% of impressions you get never had a real chance of converting. Multiply that process out by billions of ads over years, and the strategy is a good one for Amazon. But for the individual advertiser it means lower click-through and conversion rates.

Worse, every once in a while, these ads will produce a paperback sale, and this goes into your ad metrics as an ACOS many times better than it really is (because the purchase price of paperbacks is much higher than ebooks but the royalty is similar). This makes your metrics look good for the ad, when in fact they can be very, very bad.

I don't target keywords by author name or book title anymore. It's an easy way to waste money. I don't even target indie authors this way. The problem is not as bad with them, but it still exists.

All of this being the case, I target my Sponsored Product ads by choosing the product targeting option and then the individual products option, inserting the ASIN numbers of my target books. This gets me off paperbacks and displays my ad only on ebooks.

Finding relevant ASINs, and copying and pasting them into a master list is a lot of work. Quite a lot of work. But the results are worthwhile.

My impressions have been greatly reduced following this method. But these were dead impressions. My average click-through rate is now under 1 in 500 (most advisers are happy with 1 in 1000). I have plenty of ASINs that produce 1 in 100. And because these are to highly targeted books in the first place, followed by only targeting ebook editions, conversions (buys and borrows at a 1 to 2 ratio) are strong at 1.3 in 10 clicks.

These aren't cherry picked figures. These are my averages over all ads at the time of writing, including some trial ads that will likely be switched off in the future.

Don't take my word for any of this. You can put it to the test yourself. Set up an ad for one of your ebooks and target it to paperbacks by using the method above, except switch out ASIN numbers for ISBN numbers.

If you test this, like I did, you'll probably get similar results. You'll sell a majority of paperbacks, and given the true ACOS of those sales, probably not at a profit.

I've never seen these tactics, and the background reasoning for them, advised in this step detailed elsewhere. So far as I know, it's a Rob Ryan original. Try it, and tell me if it improves your ad performance. Personally, I believe this is one of the main reasons ads fail to be profitable. But fair warning, it's a lot of work in the initial stages to harvest those highly targeted ASIN numbers.

Step 5

Don't put more than a hundred keywords into the one ad. This step isn't proven, but there's growing evidence that Amazon algorithms concentrate on showing only the more successful keywords in an ad. And unless the overall ad budget is high enough, the money isn't there to serve all the keywords anyway. This is why only some keywords are chosen and others (that possibly could be good) never get off the ground.

As I say, this step isn't proven. But at the least it does no harm.

Step 6

Set an ad budget of $100.00 or more. This is another unproven theory, but it has some merit. The algorithms try to figure out which money out of all the Amazon advertisers' budgets to spend, and where and when to spend it. A higher budget sends a message you're more serious than a lower budget, and that the budget won't run out during the day. If the algorithms think the budget will run out, your ad only gets served piecemeal here and there, and probably not at those periods of the day that see the highest buyer activity and conversion rates. And yes, the time of day, day of the week, season and even phase of the moon can impact conversion rates. Look it up. It's interesting.

Some people have tried upping the budget to five, ten and even twenty-thousand dollars. I've never seen any evidence this works better than a hundred-dollar budget.

Step 7

Write good ad copy. This is like a baby blurb, and it can convert well or poorly. Essentially, the AIDA formula applies just as it does to the grown-up blurbs. Only everything is compressed.

One thing is different. Stuffing keywords into your blurb is likely a waste of time. But, for ads, there's some evidence that keywords there helps establish that critical relevancy you're after.

Go look at the ads on the books in the top 100 of the store. Count up how many advertisers use genre keywords (or author names and book titles) in their copy. Quite a lot compared to elsewhere in the store. Do those authors know something most other authors don't? Amazon sellers of other products in the store (non-book products) believe this is a factor in relevance scores. They're probably right, but I'm still researching this tactic, so I can't be sure. In the meantime, it's definitely something worth testing for yourself.

Step 8

Now that you have highly targeted ads running against keywords that are the most likely to convert, you need to optimize their performance.

No matter how well you target, you'll introduce some keywords that are duds. You think the target ASIN is a close match to your own book, but it isn't.

When do you know a dud is a dud?

Of course, there's one way to be absolutely sure. You can wait for statistically sufficient impressions. Depending on what conversion rate you think is good, you may need fifty thousand impressions and fifty clicks. Or hundreds of clicks.

The people who do this *have* to bid very low. If they don't, they'll go broke faster than a rabbit runs away from a lucky charm factory.

But advertising is *not* about getting perfect data. The quest for perfect data is a mathematician's dream but a business owner's nightmare. You'll *bleed* money on keywords that don't work.

But you don't want to work in the dark either. Quite the dilemma.

But, grasshopper, pay-per-click advertising has been around for decades. It's a multi-billion-dollar industry. Per day. There have been lots of smart minds at work on this since the pay-per-click model was born, and this is the marketer's approach they've come up with.

First, work out what sort of conversion rate you expect. This varies depending on a range of circumstances. It will be something like 1 in 10.

This is a good conversion rate. To be sure, some keywords might go 30 clicks without a conversion, and then pick up 6 in the next 30 clicks. This gives you 6 sales in 60 clicks, which is back on track.

If you killed that keyword at 30 clicks, you may have killed a good keyword.

But statistics is a double-edged sword. The above *might* be the case, but statistically your better keywords will return conversions faster than 1 in 10. These make up about 25% of your keywords (and probably most of your conversions), and they're the ones you *really* want. So, you're much less likely to kill them off by accident. As for the lesser keywords, you're still going to catch a lot of them anyway even cutting ads at, say, 20 clicks.

In addition, the click-through rate of a keyword is an indicator of relevance. If the keyword has a great CTR, leave it go a bit longer and give it more of a chance. More likely though, you'll see that most of the keywords that go 20 to 30 clicks without a conversion have also got a dud CTR.

This is the basic formula professional pay-per-click marketers use. But it's more of a benchmark. The more experienced they are, the more they'll use the CTR as a guide. And the quicker they'll terminate non-performing keywords.

You can verify this by going to YouTube and searching for "Amazon ads optimization". Pick a presenter who does this stuff for a living, and who has an ad budget of tens of thousands of dollars. More verification is Amazon itself. They tend to kill non-performing ads after just a few thousand impressions, and less than a handful of clicks. They don't wait for perfect data.

The key concept here is that you'll certainly sacrifice some good keywords. That's okay. Your aim is *profit*, not perfect data. You'll still retain most of your good keywords, and in the meantime you won't leak cash like a drunk gambler in a casino.

And if you're really, really worried about those sacrificed keywords, you can give them another chance on a different ad for a different book (assuming it's in the same subgenre etc.). If they're duds there too, kill them with fire.

Step 9

Scaling up. We all want to. We want it bad. Once we have a profitable ad, we want to start shifting those decimal points around and getting a lot more zeros on the right side of them.

But this part isn't easy. It's the hardest thing of all. It needs fuel, and that fuel is difficult to come by. And when you have it, it doesn't last. The idea is to burn it like crazy when you have the chance.

What's the fuel? It's not lots and lots of keywords. That tactic can work for a few select people in nonfiction. Not once, ever, have I seen evidence of it working for a fiction writer. Not to true scale.

Instead, this is what works. This is what you see at play on the Amazon marketplace. A book will appear all over the place, but still on *relevant* targets. It will be high up on the carousel. Probably first. It might also be on Product Display ads and Lockscreen ads. Not only will it be on relevant targets, but critically it'll be on targets with a very, very high rank.

This is where the eyeballs are. The visibility of a book with a sales rank of less than five thousand is quite high. Get on ten or twenty like that and the potential traction is more than tens of thousands of lower-ranked keywords.

Doing this isn't easy though. More accurately, it's impossible unless one criterion is met. You can bid as high as you like, and you *still* won't meet that criterion. And that criterion is a high sales rank for the book you're advertising.

It works like this. The books with a stellar sales rank have enormous potential to generate sales for books advertised on them. Smart advertisers know this. The advertising spots on those books are fought over by authors like hyenas tearing apart a carcass. Sorry for the imagery, but it's *accurate* imagery. You won't get a place at that grisly feast unless you bid pretty high. *And* you've seeded relevance. Then you're in with a real chance.

There might only be ten or twenty books like that in an entire subgenre at one time. But there are thousands of advertisers bidding for places at the dinner table. How is Amazon to determine which few to invite, and which of the masses to reject?

Higher bids are a factor. Relevance is a factor. You need those things. They're essential. But thousands of authors have those things too, and there's space for only a few. And Amazon, being client-centric, wants to put the books in front of customers that they're most likely to buy.

How do they determine the books most likely to be bought? By looking at what *is* being bought.

If a book you're trying to advertise has a sales rank of less than, say, 1000, Amazon *knows* it's selling. And it's selling right now. Assuming relevance and a high enough bid, that book is going to get preferential treatment over books with a worse rank.

Like everything else Amazon does, it rewards sales. I've had sales ranks of below 1,000, and the traction you get at that level with ads is *awesome*. There's nothing like it. Day after day, week after week, those ads convert, and they convert at scale.

But nothing lasts forever. Sales rank decreases over time, and with it your traction on whichever books are currently performing at a high level.

Did you really think Amazon would let you buy your way to the top of the store just by advertising? They don't. The better you sell, the more they reward you with ad placement.

This is why so many people have trouble scaling. Selling well in the first place is the pre-requisite. It's also why the best time to advertise is when you have a new release. That's your best chance of a high rank. It's why other sites such as BookBub are so handy for a launch. They give you rank.

At least, those sorts of promotions give you rank for a short while. Your Amazon ads will perform correspondingly. But to sustain that rank, and to sustain the scaled Amazon ads, you need to "stick" at a high rank organically.

This whole concept ties in with the myth of dying ads. If an ad was actually performing, but has gone off the boil, what's a bet your sales rank has slid as well? This is the root cause.

When that happens the standard advice is to switch the ad off and start a new one. This is *catastrophically* bad advice. You've built relevance on that ad. You've converted off it. Amazon doesn't forget. If you pump life into your sales rank again via some sort of a promotion, that ad will flare back to life.

There you have it. That's how to scale. It's not easy though.

All of this is just the briefest outline of how to make money off Amazon ads. Still, I think I've given you an awful lot to digest.

Have I not?

If you want more, and there's *much* more, stay tuned. That book, like the one on blurbs, is on the way.

14. Is There a Future for Indie Publishing?

Predictions are in vain. So I'm not going to make any. But that doesn't mean I won't deduce a few things.

People worry about the millions and millions of new books flooding Amazon each year. I referenced this myself in the introduction to this book.

But is it really such a huge issue? Will there be so many books that it'll be impossible to gain traction?

That growing flood of new books isn't really a problem. Sadly, most of these new authors will be operating under a lack of correct knowledge. Many will take little time to study the marketplace and learn successful strategies. Others will take the time, but they'll listen to those who offer standard advice rather than *best practice*. Or worse, they'll listen to just plain bad advice. There's lots of it out there. You can buy it by the truckload.

Correct knowledge and hard work will keep you ahead of the pack. You don't need to worry about the masses if you're always seeking best practice and evaluating advice with a cool, rational attitude. Not to mention researching it afterwards instead of accepting it at face value.

But with the teeming masses come two smaller groups of writers, and they can, and will, outsell you if you give them the chance. They have their right to reach for the sun as well, so good luck to them. In the end, the winners will be the ones, old or new, who put in the hard work and develop the best publishing skillset. And that's how it should be, yes?

The first group is that band of new writers who have never tried to become traditionally published. They've set their eyes on the indie approach from the outset, and they know the lifestyle and financial rewards it can bring. They haven't published yet, but they're building up a backlist in preparedness. And they're sharpening their business, publishing and marketing skills the way a cat plays with a mouse. They seek out the best advice, and they use their own judgement, which gets sharper every day, to reject the bad advice that the masses will swallow whole. These writers will hit the ground running when they click the publish button.

The second group is made up of traditionally published authors. More and more of them will make the jump to indie publishing as their royalties from the big publishing houses continue to dwindle. And they have a lot of craft and skill behind them. Not as indies, but they'll learn that just the same way the first group will.

The rest of the oncoming wave of new authors, either coming direct to indie publishing or via traditional publishing, will follow standard advice. They'll get left behind.

It's that much, much smaller group who'll seek out and labor under correct knowledge that'll swamp you out of sales if you let them.

Don't let them. *Be one of them instead.*

What else does the future of indie publishing hold? The same thing that's in store for the rest of the world: the rise, and then the towering rise, of the subscription model.

Amazon already has Kindle Unlimited. When it started, most authors were getting a lot more buys than borrows. Then it evened out. Now? Most people have a borrow to buy ratio of two to one. Some genres are experiencing much higher ratios.

And Amazon promotes KU heavily. They *want* people in KU. And judging by how many people subscribe, and the massive growth KU has experienced, people *want* to be in it.

As it happens, I like KU. I think it offers benefits to indie authors. Not all authors love it though. Some hate it.

None of that matters.

KU is here, and all indications are that it's not only going to stay, but that it's barely begun yet. It'll grow much, much bigger. Within a few years the ratio of borrows to sales might be five to one.

I base this on two factors. Firstly, the massive growth KU has already seen in a few short years. Secondly, on what's happening all around us. Everything is subscription these days. I'm typing this on Microsoft Word, for which I have a subscription. Want to watch a movie tonight? You'll probably see it on Netflix. I could keep going, but the following statistic says it all. The subscription ecommerce market has increased by more than 100% a year for the past five years. That's a *massive* upward trend. As usual, for verification, Google something like "growth of ecommerce subscription services".

Now, there's a ceiling to this growth. At some point it'll reach a point of stagnation. Where will that point be for KU? It's probably got at *least* a few more years to go at the same rate that it's been going. This means a borrow to buy ratio of at least five to one, possibly ten to one or more.

It's up to us to deal with it, whether we like KU or not. KU lowers our payout per book. But it increases it by gaining us readers we wouldn't have otherwise had. But that's a passive way of looking at things. It's reactionary. It's not how you get ahead of the curve.

The way to get ahead of the curve is to analyze your current business model, and ask if it'll still stand up in a world where borrows massively outweigh sales.

For instance, do you rely on permafree as a strategy? If so, KU will erode your earnings. Do you write short books and release infrequently? Are you struggling to afford advertising because the return on investment isn't good on short books? Is your read-through rate from book one in a series to the rest less than 80%? All these things will undermine your position as KU expands.

My advice is to find any weaknesses you have in craft, marketing and copywriting now. Fix them. If you don't, the growth of KU will gnaw away at your income relentlessly.

You may not be in KU. But does that mean you're immune to these problems? Probably not. At some stage, the industry will reach a turning point. KU popularity will grow so much that it'll send the other retailers out of business. Or they'll try to keep their market share by setting up their own subscription service. (That's my bet.) Either way, being wide is no protection. Either way, learning the craft of marketing will give you an edge in the super-competitive environment to come.

The other great challenge will be the cost of pay-per-click advertising. Does anyone believe bid prices (on any of the platforms that authors use) will come down? Does anyone think they've peaked and will hold steady?

I don't believe either of those things. The cost of advertising will go up. As publishers, we can moan about it, or we can look for ways to profit from it anyway.

And you *can* profit from pay-per-click advertising, especially on Amazon ads, even when the bids are high. I've shown some strategies in this book to do so. The key is understanding how the ads work. Once you grasp that, then anything is possible.

Want to launch a book? There are ways to do so profitably. Want to breathe life back into an old series that's faded away? Ads can do that too.

This is a field where tactics change rapidly. Amazon in particular is altering their system. We have a new dashboard now, and it comes with better metrics. We now have ad-generated page reads reported. Some ad types have disappeared. New ones are offered. Amazon doesn't stand still for long. But the point here is that they're getting better. They're offering us a better service.

Why?

As always, when you dig deep you find answers.

Amazon is improving their advertising platform for two reasons. One, they want you to spend your advertising dollars with them instead of their competition – BookBub and Facebook. Two, they're getting ready for what's to come. And what's to come will increasingly be a pay-to-play world. Even the big dogs in indie publishing have felt the beginning of this new wave. Their sales (and borrows) have dropped. More and more they need to advertise to retain the revenue stream they were accustomed to.

As with the tsunami of new books on Amazon, correct knowledge of how to run PPC ads is what will see you surf the wave rather than be overwhelmed by it.

In short, nothing about publishing is getting easier. Everything is getting harder. But the rewards are still there in abundance for those who put in the work and develop the required skillsets.

15. A Candid Appraisal of Indie Resources

This isn't a comprehensive list. It's just a few comments about the resources I've used, or had cause to look into.

One note before we begin. When evaluating a source of information on publishing, check to see how long ago they published themselves, or if they even publish at all. Check their sales rank, too. There are advisers out there who haven't published for years, don't sell when they do and yet still charge lots of money for books and courses purporting to teach you how to sell books…

Mark Dawson

Mark Dawson is probably the highest profile indie author in the world. He transformed from a lawyer into an author. And then from an author into a mega author. Not satisfied with that, he transformed again into an educational powerhouse providing mainstream media interviews and training courses for indie authors.

I've never taken his courses, so I can't comment on their quality. Judging from the free material that he releases now and then, the quality is good. That's certainly the reputation those courses have in the indie community as well. In short, the trust factor is high. It did get tarnished though in July 2020 when he acknowledged buying 400 copies of his own book to reach the Top 10 of the *Sunday Times*. His Top 10 position was later stripped. This is a fairly common practice, but that defense wasn't well received by everybody.

I'm not the indie police, so make up your own minds about him. My advice to him though (as if he needs any from me) is to be uber careful in the future. Both of what he does, and those he associates with, especially to deliver his training. Trust is given for free, but once broken not all the money in the world can buy it back.

He runs a Facebook group (Self Publishing Formula) which can be useful.

There's also a podcast. I have to say, I've only ever caught a few minutes of this now and then. I'd much, much rather read a book or a blogpost than devote the time to listen to a podcast. Life is too short for that. But that's probably just me.

There's also a website with a blog and access to other resources for free. These are all good for the beginner. Safe to say, the more advanced material is in his courses which must be paid for. And that's fair enough.

Bryan Cohen

Bryan has a reputation as a copywriter. He says in the beginning of his book, *How to Write A Sizzling Synopsis*, that his copywriting career started around 2009 and that he wrote thousands of articles for blogs before becoming a ghostwriter. Over these years he put in his 10,000 hours of Malcolm Gladwellesque copywriting expertise.

I don't understand this. Writing articles for blogs and ghostwriting is creating content. The official term for a person who does that is "content writer". Fiction and nonfiction authors, as well as bloggers, are content writers. Copywriting is a specialist skillset involving writing sales copy, publicity material and persuasive documents. I'd like to know his background in *this*, rather than content writing, to judge his actual copywriting experience.

If you're in doubt about the huge difference between content writing and copywriting, Googling the meaning of those terms would explain things in detail. In short, content writing entertains or informs. Copywriting sells.

Bryan is also one of the chief proponents of the "buy" CTA at the end of a blurb.

Most importantly, he runs a blurb-writing business (Best Page Forward) that indies use. At the time of writing, the fee for this is $297.00. This isn't cheap. On the other hand, sometimes you only get what you pay for. If any of you are considering this service, it would be prudent, as with hiring anyone for any job, to ask for relevant qualifications. In this case, details of Bryan's actual copywriting background.

If you're satisfied that he's a genuinely good copywriter, you have the additional option of signing up on Teachable for Best Page Forward's copywriting course. It costs $10,000.

David Gaughran

I don't think anyone has done more for the industry than David Gaughran. His nonfiction books are, in my view, the best primers on being indie that exist. They're comprehensive, up-to-date and just plain chock-full of valuable insights for anyone trying to figure out the basics of indie publishing. The only one I haven't read is his book on BookBub advertising. (The only reason I haven't read it is because I do pretty well with BookBub advertising myself. If not, I'd pick it up in a flash).

But he doesn't stop at the books. He runs a blog and YouTube channel too, which I find useful. And no one has done more to expose the bad actors, scammers and pretenders that plague our industry than he has. I'm sure this isn't easy. It's a difficult path to tread because there's a risk those same bad actors will turn around and target him. I admire his guts for taking that on.

Chris Fox

Chris Fox is a successful author. He has a good balance of fiction and nonfiction books in his backlist. His nonfiction books are targeted squarely at indie authors.

He also has a website with writer resources. To be sure, I don't agree with everything he says, but most of it is good. His views on profiling a target audience don't resonate with me. It's a good marketing principle in several ways, but not apt for many situations. Specifically, it's not apt for a lot of genres in the publishing world.

He also runs a YouTube channel on all things author related. What I especially like about this is that he takes time to interact with his viewers in the comments and answer questions. He's also transparent with his sales figures and advertising costs.

The 20Booksto50K Facebook group

Lots of successful authors post here, and the overall attitude is good. The administrators work hard to keep the group positive, open and free of drama. On the downside, there are so many posts on so many subjects that it's hard to keep track of things. Personally, I also find the many posts that have nothing to do with book marketing, and which sometimes choke the feed, quite annoying.

Brian Meeks

Brian has several nonfiction books directed at indie authors. One is on Amazon ads and the other on copywriting for blurbs. Matching these are two Facebook groups on the same topics.

His background is data analysis. But data analysis and marketing are two very separate fields. I hold the opposite view to him on nearly every point when it comes to Amazon ads.

He abandoned a fantasy series despite a rapid release strategy and a BookBub featured deal. (10 books were planned, a month apart, but only five were ever released.)

Brian places emphasis on gathering perfect data, or at least to strive for it. But pay-per-click advertising has been around for decades. There's a body of best practice established via testing. Its drive is toward profit, not perfect data. There are many resources on this. They follow the same pattern of specific targeting rather than spaghetti-on-the-wall, an acceptance that relevance is vital, adequate bids and terminating underperforming keywords *well* before the point of statistically perfect data.

Brian doesn't advocate any of those things.

He's also ventured into copywriting, and published a book on the subject. He's the other chief proponent of the buy CTA at the end of a blurb. He's on record, however, acknowledging it doesn't sell more books. He says readers expect it though (because many ads do end with a buy CTA) and it acts as a signpost. To be honest, I can't follow his logic. But I will say this. I don't think readers expect it at all. How could they, when traditional publishers don't use them in blurbs and only one in something like a thousand (maybe 10,000) indies do?

He acknowledges that he has no background in copywriting, and that he's self-taught after reading *The Adweek Copywriting Handbook*. He never references any other books or training.

There's a *vast* body of copywriting theory available. It takes most people five years of ardent study to acquire a big chunk of that knowledge and learn how to employ it profitably in practice.

Apart from a handful of sentences, he doesn't discuss copywriting theory in his blurb book. I found that a major disappointment. Instead, it comprises mostly blurbs written by other authors and posted in his Facebook group or emailed to him for critique. Each blurb is repeated with the variation in wording he suggests.

I admire his ingenuity here in bulking out a book with examples by copying and pasting. But I would have preferred a whole lot less of that and a whole lot more discussion about the many, many copywriting tactics and strategies and how they apply to blurbs. But that's just me.

I also admire his supreme self-belief. It really is incredible. He's a data analyst, but he has the confidence to teach people Amazon ads, copywriting, and to run a blurb-writing service for $150.00 a pop. He turns his hand to nonfiction and fiction. He writes noir mystery, humor, epic fantasy, suspense, thrillers and even basketball.

It's clear that he never suffers the debilitating effects of imposter syndrome. Good for him!

Kboards Writers' Cafe

This was once the premier place for indie authors, but most of the successful authors who used to post there have moved to Facebook groups. If you're still a member, be careful who you listen to. Most of the advice on selling books comes from people who aren't selling books. And moderator censorship is extremely high.

Writer Sanctum

The new kid on the block. It's well organized, and posts on various specific subjects are easy to find. I prefer it to Kboards. Moderation is also far less intrusive – meaning you're much freer to say what you think. Even so, internet forums on the whole have lost ground to Facebook groups.

Authors Optimizing Amazon and Facebook Ads

This is one of the best Facebook groups. They take the mainstream pay-per-click marketing approach rather than adhere to the Brian Meeks data analysis school of thought, and good advice is generously given by group members.

I shouldn't recommend it, because they're the competition to my own Facebook group (more on that in a moment) but I do anyway. Some very successful authors hang out there.

Nicholas Erik

Nicholas has a guide (available if you subscribe) and several books for indie authors. He also runs courses.

I haven't taken any of these. But I've seen some of the free videos via his newsletter. The information he gives, especially relating to launches and PPC advertising, is solid. He's also very open with what's worked and hasn't worked for him. All in all, a trustworthy resource. He's in the trenches, actually making a living as a fiction author rather than making a living just teaching it. There's a difference. In fact, all the difference in the world.

16. A Facebook Group to Seek out Best Practice

We've covered a lot of ground together. But at the beating heart of this book has always been one guiding belief: success stems from questioning standard advice and striving for best practice.

And best practice, like the truth, is out there. But no one person understands it all. Still less do people share. When they discover a nugget of gold, they tend to keep it to themselves.

There's another way. Often writers *do* share. I've been fortunate in my career, and I've come across a number of people like that. I've benefited from their generosity. They're one of the reasons I can write for a living.

And so, I run a Facebook group in that spirit. Its name?

Author Unleashed

Join me there. It's closing in on 2,000 members. Many are bestsellers. Some are Top 100 sellers. There are some famous indie names in that group, and they share their knowledge. Our motto is this: Dig deep. Find the truth. Question standard practice – seek *best* practice.

Together, we're a group that shares knowledge among ourselves freely. It's a place to get feedback on blurbs and Amazon ads until they're honed to razor-like effectiveness. It's a place to discuss, discover and even drive the cutting edge of marketing for indie authors.

Want to be part of that? I look forward to meeting you.

Here we are. At the end.

I've talked a lot about business in this book. It is, after all, a marketing book. I've used terms such as "prospect" instead of "reader". But don't let that mislead you. I'm an artist. I love nothing more than to paint a picture with words. I think there's no nobler art than that of the storyteller.

But this book will be judged on its merits. It'll be judged by how well it did its job of giving you, the reader, information to help you on your writer's journey.

What I *hate* after reading a book like this is the feeling that it was stuffed with irrelevant and useless padding. What I *hate* is if the information I paid for was freely available elsewhere on blogs and the like.

If I've done those things to you, I deserve a review bomb.

On the other hand, if I've filled each chapter with good information that'll help your career, and I've given you a perspective on things that you haven't seen elsewhere, and most especially, if I've given you that correct knowledge that will guide your labor, then I'd like to know that. Tell me in the reviews on Amazon. Tell me if this is a good book.

What the experts say is that I'm supposed to insert a link here to make it easy for you to leave a review. They're not wrong. But I'm not going to do that. You know how to leave one if I've helped you.

The choice, as always, is yours.

I went into a lot of detail on blurbs in this book. But I only scratched the surface. I love blurbs. I love copywriting. I know stuff. All that has come together in book two of this series – *Book Blurbs Unleashed*. My aim was to make it the *definitive* guide, ever, on blurbs. I've left no stone unturned, and many, many things will surprise you.

Interested? It's out now.

Book three is *Amazon Ads Unleashed*. Again, for all that I've given you a blueprint for success in this book, that guide will take you to the next level. Check out the reviews, and you'll see what I mean.

Thanks for reading. And as always, keep digging for the truth!

Made in the USA
Las Vegas, NV
02 February 2023

66797324R00069